The Importance of Campaign Promises

Campaign promises are a cornerstone of representative democracy. Candidates make promises to signal to voters their intentions in office, and voters evaluate candidates based on those promises. This study unpacks the theorized pathway regarding campaign promises; not whether promises are kept but what purpose promises serve, what they signal, and how they affect voter decision-making. The author explores the pathways and conditions influencing promises and finds that promises tend to have a polarizing effect on voters' opinions of politicians, attracting similarly positioned voters and strongly repelling voters who disagree with a candidate's position. In addition, voters perceive promise breakers as less honest and less likely to follow through than candidates who took the same position but more weakly. With a wealth of data and fascinating case studies, this book is full of important insights into electoral psychology and the study of promises, campaigning, and representation.

Tabitha Bonilla is Assistant Professor in Human Development and Social Policy and Political Science and Faculty Fellow in the Institute for Policy Research at Northwestern University.

The Importance of Campaign Promises

TABITHA BONILLA

Northwestern University

CAMBRIDGE
UNIVERSITY PRESS

CAMBRIDGE
UNIVERSITY PRESS

University Printing House, Cambridge CB2 8BS, United Kingdom

One Liberty Plaza, 20th Floor, New York, NY 10006, USA

477 Williamstown Road, Port Melbourne, VIC 3207, Australia

314–321, 3rd Floor, Plot 3, Splendor Forum, Jasola District Centre, New Delhi – 110025, India

103 Penang Road, #05–06/07, Visioncrest Commercial, Singapore 238467

Cambridge University Press is part of the University of Cambridge.

It furthers the University's mission by disseminating knowledge in the pursuit of education, learning, and research at the highest international levels of excellence.

www.cambridge.org
Information on this title: www.cambridge.org/9781108843331
DOI: 10.1017/9781108910170

First published 2022

A catalogue record for this publication is available from the British Library.

Library of Congress Cataloging-in-Publication Data
NAMES: Bonilla, Tabitha, author.
TITLE: The importance of campaign promises / Tabitha Bonilla.
DESCRIPTION: New York, N.Y. : Cambridge University Press, 2021. |
Includes bibliographical references and index.
IDENTIFIERS: LCCN 2021025010 (print) | LCCN 2021025011 (ebook) |
ISBN 9781108843331 (hardback) | ISBN 9781108824248 (paperback) |
ISBN 9781108910170 (epub)
SUBJECTS: LCSH: Campaign promises–United States. | Communication in politics–United States. | Rhetoric–Political aspects–United States. |
Presidential candidates–United States–Public opinion. |
Presidents–United States–Election–History–20th century. |
Presidents–United States–Election–History–21st century. |
BISAC: POLITICAL SCIENCE / American Government / General |
POLITICAL SCIENCE / American Government / General
CLASSIFICATION: LCC JK1976 .B66 2021 (print) | LCC JK1976 (ebook) |
DDC 324.70973–dc23
LC record available at https://lccn.loc.gov/2021025010
LC ebook record available at https://lccn.loc.gov/2021025011

ISBN 978-1-108-84333-1 Hardback

For my family

Contents

Figures

List of Figures

Tables

Acknowledgments

This book started as a small idea sparked from a conversation about machine learning, campaign speech, and voter behavior during a rather unremarkable dinner. Moving from that wildly outrageous idea to a complete book has been a fascinating, sometimes fun, and long endeavor. As with any book that begins as a dissertation, my committee played an invaluable role in shaping my thoughts on campaign promises through their questions, advice, and guidance. I am grateful for the help and attention given to this work by my committee, Mike Tomz, Justin Grimmer, and Paul Sniderman. I particularly appreciate Mike and Paul's work to create the Laboratory for the Study of American Values through which the core data was collected. I also greatly appreciate the time and effort that Mike gave to help me turn this idea into a dissertation, and his insights helped me push through at critical junctures in this work. Thanks to Jon Krosnick for his help in coding the debates and for access to research assistants.

After arriving at Northwestern University, Jamie Druckman offered invaluable mentorship, commenting on several drafts and organizing a Chicago-based book conference. I appreciate learning from Jamie; this book would not be what it is without his help and support. I am also grateful to Petia Kostadinova who read the entire manuscript and offered comments on additional chapters, as well as answered several questions through email at various times through the process. Petia Kostadinova, Mary McGrath, Ethan Busby, Sam Gubitz, Adam Howat, Matt Nelson, Kumar Ramanathan, and Jake Rothschild all gave feedback during my book conference, and I appreciate their thoughtful comments. Several individuals also helped me refine arguments and gave important and proactive feedback at conferences and workshops, which

I hope to have thoughtfully incorporated. They included Elin Naurin, Dennis Chong, Christian Grose, and Timothy Ryan. Additionally, I am grateful to Kate Epstein, who has taught me so much about the craft of writing. Thank-you as well to those who made Northwestern and Chicagoland a community while I finished this book, including Al Tillery, Julie Lee Merseth, Mary McGrath, Laurel Harbridge, and Alexandra Filindra. I also appreciate Pa Nhia Vang, Erin PonTell, Dora Duru, Dylan Kennedy, and Joseph Kim for their research assistance. Access to feedback and research funds was provided through Stanford Graduate Research Office, EDGE-SBE (Enhancing Diversity in Graduate Education–Social and Behavioral Sciences), Northwestern Political Science Research Lab, Undergraduate Research Assistance Program, and Institute for Policy Research.

While some have directly supported my thinking and writing process on this book, others have supported me in other critical ways. Thank-you to Krystale Littlejohn, Natalie Mendoza, Rebecca Neri, and Martha Balaguera, who kept me accountable and writing; Martha had the bright idea to work on our most frustrating tasks in virtual community, and our writing sessions have helped so much. Thank-you to a number of folks at MIT who encouraged me to pursue graduate school and an academic career, and whose advice helped me along the way. Chappell Lawson helped me reach the conclusion that political science research was what I really wanted to do. Christopher Jones, Blanche Staton, and Karl Reid helped give me an insight into academic life and taught me how to get there and get through. And a special thank-you to Sandy Tenorio, whose encouragement and kindness helped me through my undergraduate studies and who has kept in touch all these years.

My parents, Victor and Leslie, whose drive, faith, and emphasis on education gave me the opportunity to write this book – I appreciate your prayers, hugs, and encouragement. And I am grateful to my siblings – Tasha, Joshua, Caleb, Nikki, Erica, Seth, Samuel, Ariel, Israel, and Joel – some of whom offered advice, pretested surveys, and proofread early drafts, and mostly kept me sane. I am also appreciative to Shawan Worsley, my sister-in-law, whose insights and advice as a friend and former academic have lifted me up.

A final round of thank-yous to my partner and children for grounding me. My three daughters, Micah, Ava, and Thea, grew along with this project. They propelled me forward with their love, laughter, and curiosity, and displayed remarkable patience throughout this process – especially as I spent several weeks editing this manuscript through a global pandemic. Finally, to my husband and partner, Marcelo, I am deeply thankful for both emotional and technical support. I am grateful for the long hours spent helping me debug Python and hearing me talk out my ideas. I also appreciate the camaraderie and support that you brought as a fellow graduate student, and now assistant professor. I appreciate the perspective that you have given me when I have needed it most.

PART I

WHY AND HOW PROMISES MATTER

I

A Closer Look at Campaign Promises

Donald Trump may have been considered an unconventional candidate for president and his rhetoric unusual in many ways, but his candidacy clearly illustrates the nuances of how candidates take positions. Over the course of his campaign, he made several very clear promises that were strong statements about how he would act if elected. For example, "I will build a great wall," he promised. "And nobody builds walls better than me, believe me – and I'll build them very inexpensively. I will build a great, great wall on our southern border, and I will make Mexico pay for that wall. Mark my words" (Johnson, 2016). On getting rid of the Affordable Care Act, banning Syrian refugees, strengthening the military, and many more issues, Trump was firm and clear both on how he would act and that he would act on these issues as president. Not only did he address the public with right-leaning positions, but he attached an action (and sometimes an outcome) to them. Polls indicate that support for Trump rose quickly after he entered the presidential race and retained leadership throughout the Republican primaries (Craighill and Clement, 2015). Even if Trump supporters did not necessarily believe that he would exactly realize all of the promises he had made, some indicated belief that the status quo would shift toward Trump's promised outcomes (Azevedo, Jost, and Rothmund, 2017).[1]

While Trump made definitive stances on immigration policies and the Affordable Care Act, on other issues he showed less resolution.

[1] Certainly elections are quite partisan and many Republicans supported the Republican nominee for partisan reasons. But many anecdotes tell of voters who thought that even if Trump's promises weren't realized, the status quo would more closely shift to their ideal policy outcome.

For example, he demonstrated significant shape-shifting (Saward, 2014) in his stance on banning abortion. As a private citizen, Trump had long seemed to be pro-choice (Keneally, 2016). However, as a Republican candidate, Trump revealed that he was opposed to abortion but was inclined to maintain the status quo because, as he told a reporter, "[t]he laws are set now on abortion and that's the way they're going to remain until they're changed" (Bump, 2016). Even when under fire from pro-life groups and amid accusations that he could not be an effective candidate for the GOP without a more decisive promise of action, Trump made no promises about abortion (DelReal, 2016). His statements suggested a changing position on abortion policy, but Trump never committed to any policy stances on abortion as a candidate.[2] Whether it was because of his lack of credibility on the issue, personal convictions, or some other reason, Trump clearly avoided doing more than assuring voters that he was not pro-choice. He also refused to make any promises on social issues such as same-sex marriage and protections for LGBTQ+ individuals, as did other GOP candidates (Eaton, 2016). He described his beliefs or general sentiments but refrained from bold assurances of what he would do in the future.

Trump's campaign stances in 2016 exemplify the wide range of methods that many candidates use to introduce their positions to voters, and other contenders for public office make similar choices. In some cases, candidates illustrate positions and couple them with promises that they will act on those positions. In other circumstances, candidates take a position on an issue but refrain from indicating that they will do something because of that position. The public was responsive to the various ways Trump stated his positions – whether they were too strong or not strong enough – and it seems much of the public response was based on reactions to the strengths (or weaknesses) of his positions applied by his language. In general, how do these distinctions in describing positions affect the way that voters perceive candidates? In particular, how do promises affect voter evaluations? Because promissory representation is a basic conception of democratic representation, this is a critical question to understand,

---

[2] At one point in the campaign, Trump stated that he "believed" women should be punished for getting abortions, but he did not follow through by suggesting that he would work to enact legislation that would do so. His campaign also quickly walked back those comments (Bump, 2016).

and while there is work on understanding both how issues matter to voters and how promises are fulfilled, there is need to further investigate how promises affect voter decision-making.

This book extends our knowledge both of candidate communication and promises by considering what candidates communicate to voters beyond revealing their positions, and it deepens our understanding of how position-taking is more nuanced than candidates simply selecting an issue stance. The theory and the data presented here furthers our understanding of candidate positions and promissory representation by investigating what candidates communicate to voters by making a promise. Finally, the book also builds on an important literature on promise fulfillment to investigate how voters understand and use those promises to evaluate candidates.

To be sure, past research establishes that promises matter to voters (Naurin, 2014). That voters use promises to select and hold elected officials accountable is a central tenet of conceptions of the foundational theories of promissory representation (Mansbridge, 2003). Indeed, promises matter to voters both prospectively, for the campaigns in which candidates make promises, and retrospectively, for assessments of elected officials whose accountability can be appraised by fulfilled promises. While there is a decent understanding of portions of each of these representative pathways, the specific and particular effect of promises remains underexplored. Prospectively, much work has considered how candidate-positioning affects voter behavior, and candidate rhetoric is undeniably important to voter judgments of candidates (Vavreck, 2009; Riker, 1996). The specific role of promises has been heavily theorized, but the actual effect of promises themselves is yet to be empiricized. Retrospectively, much of the focus is on promise fulfillment and accountability (Mansbridge, 2009; Thomson et al., 2017) but not on how and why promises signal information that changes the retrospective judgments of candidates. When promises themselves are discussed, voters indeed view them as mechanisms to select and hold elected officials accountable but with a richer understanding of what that may mean and how voters view promises as fulfilled (Naurin, 2014).

In the remainder of this chapter, I clarify what I mean when I refer to campaign promises and give a rationale for this definition. I then explain why it is important to reconsider promise-making and the implications of considering a more nuanced definition of promises in voter selection pathways. Finally, I detail how the rest of this book demonstrates the importance of campaign promises and why understanding them yields crucial implications for normative formulations of promissory representation.

1.1 WHAT ARE CAMPAIGN PROMISES?

As a starting point to understanding promise-making, in terms of both how candidates use promises and how voters perceive promises, I propose a clear definition of campaign promises that is critical to the argument of this book. In step with other investigators of campaign promises, I define a promise as a position statement on a policy issue that explicitly indicates an action a candidate will take if elected to office or identifies a political outcome as a result of the candidate's election.[3] This means that I ignore candidate statements about their own character or non-policy actions. I also ignore the statements of elected officials serving in office unless they are seeking an office they do not currently hold. Of course, since most politicians aim to run for reelection, elected officials who are currently serving a term could also be considered candidates running for office. However, they have already had a chance to fulfill campaign promises and voter calculations reflect that, making campaign promises less important. Thus all candidate discussions in this book pertain to the unknown possibility of what might happen if a candidate is elected to a new position.

Candidate promises can take a wide variety of forms. For instance, they might make promises to enact specific policies when entering office, as Bill Clinton did in announcing his candidacy for the presidential primaries in 1991, when he "pledg[ed] to the American people that in the first year of a Clinton Administration, [he would] present a plan to Congress and the American people to provide affordable, quality health care for all

---

[3] This definition is quite similar to the ones that scholars from Royed (1996) to Thomson et al. (2017) have used. Because I am primarily interested in the subjective opinions associated with prospective promise-making and less concerned with establishing an objective task of promise fulfillment, I have not referenced the ability to measure the outcome of a promise. Key differences between the different definitions are detailed in Chapter 2.

Americans" (Clinton, 1991).[4] The use of the term "pledge," as promissory language, may have strengthened the weight of the promise in swaying voters. But candidates can promise without using words such as promise, pledge, guarantee, or "to read my lips." For instance, Democratic Senate candidate Thomas Dixon told voters, "The first thing that I would do [about gun violence] is pushing to close those loopholes that allow [guns] to get into hands that they're not supposed to" (Dixon, 2016). Candidates also use promises to emphasize their commitment to toeing a party line as Republican presidential contender Senator Marco Rubio did, saying "we will protect the Second Amendment when I'm president of the United States" (Rubio, 2015).[5]

On the other hand, when candidates take positions on issues without making assurances about how they will act in the future, I treat these as non-promise policy statements rather than promises. For example, candidates may give their opinion but refrain from suggesting that they themselves might act on it. For example, presidential candidate John Kasich said, "I'm in favor of [defining] marriage between … a man and a woman" (Kasich, 2015). Similarly, in the 2002 Texas Senatorial debates, candidate John Cornyn suggested he was broadly supportive of the war on drugs, but only offered that "*maybe* we need to do more surveillance … to make sure that kids don't come into contact with drug dealers" (Cornyn, 2002). As with promises, non-promise statements

---

4 Along with a plan to fix the economy and close the budget deficit, providing universal health care to the American public was a key tenet of Clinton's campaign (Matalin, Carville, and Knobler, 1994). At the time, 79 percent of Americans wanted to see drastic change in the health-care system and over half wanted a government insurance plan (Miller, Kinder, and Rosenstone, 1999), but there was no clear indication that Clinton's plan could come to fruition if he was elected. Indeed, the public was widely divided on how best to fix health care. Yet, the voting public understood from this promise that Clinton cared about health care and would act on it in office. According to Clinton's campaign manager, James Carville, the emphasis on health care was an important strategic move in order to indicate to voters that Clinton was addressing their concerns in a real and tangible way, and it helped Clinton win the election (Matalin, Carville, and Knobler, 1994).

5 Candidates also make promises about outcomes that are not necessarily relevant from a policy standpoint. For instance, promises to uphold particular values (honesty or fidelity) have little relevance to policy discussions. While perhaps all types of promises matter to voter evaluations in some way, in this book I focus on how policy-relevant campaign promises sway voter opinions. Since it is a novel contribution to consider how promises differentiate from other types of policy statements, I leave room to consider more variations on promises to future work.

can reflect values candidates seek to project and beliefs that are not necessarily relevant from a policy standpoint. In the same Senatorial debate, candidate John Cornyn said, "I believe we ought to do better" at reaching across the aisle.[6] Other candidates have indicated values, such as honesty, that they believe to be important but that are not directly tied to policy stances. While these types of value statements may also cause voters to react differently to candidates, they are also beyond the scope of this book.

The question arising from the distinction between promises and non-promise policy statements is how voters react to divergences between the language shaping positions. In discussing how voters choose representation based on a candidate's position, political scientists conventionally view any type of position statement as an equal indicator of what candidates will do in office. The result is the, perhaps unintentional, normative assumption that any position statement on policy is equivalent, whether it is a promise or not. I argue that voters nonetheless react differently to promises and non-promises, and that these affect evaluations of candidates differently. I base this in part on the research of linguist John Austin, who demonstrates in his theory of performative utterances that promise statements indicate sentiments on a topic (for instance commitment), but they cannot be proven true or false in the moment (Austin, 1975). As performative utterances, promises are the principal-agent problem theorists have long used to define how voters choose representatives of democracy (Mansbridge, 2003). Candidates make a statement to express where they stand on a particular issue, but voters cannot weight the veracity of a candidate's statement until the voter sees the candidate act. But linguist Paul Grice (1991) demonstrates that people distinguish between promises and non-promises – between "what is said, what is conventionally implicated, and what is nonconventionally implicated" (p. 41). In this book, I consider what is "nonconventionally implicated" when candidates promise, and demonstrate that voters view candidates differently based on the type of statement they make. As Chong and Druckman (2011) note, "When speakers choose their words strategically ... recipients of such information may have an incentive to process it differently" (p. 17). I demonstrate that even the subtle distinction between promise and non-promise

---

[6] If Cornyn had explicitly linked this to a policy, it would be part of a promise statement; generally, however, reaching across the aisle does not explain what a candidate will do on policy.

statements conveys important information to voters about the candidate and how the candidate will represent their constituents.

The difference between promises and non-promises, I argue, is that promises imply a stronger commitment to an issue than a non-promise statement. Because of this, promises yield a difference in voter opinions of the candidate who makes them. Voters can never be sure how candidates will act once elected. In many situations, individuals reduce uncertainty about future events by creating larger costs for acting out of character (Vanberg, 2008; Charness and Dufwenberg, 2006). Promises should increase candidate likelihood of adhering to a position because they increase costs of shifting to a new position (Saward, 2014). Ultimately, candidates who promise should be much more attractive to like-minded voters.

1.2 UNDERSTANDING HOW PROMISES AFFECTS VOTERS MATTERS FOR UNDERSTANDING REPRESENTATION

The primary contribution of this book is to clarify the conceptualization of promissory representation and provide empirics to a long-theorized process. This contribution takes four distinct forms. First, I offer an important clarification that is empirically relevant for how candidates act and deliver their positions. Though many researchers have examined how candidate's positions affect voting, much of this work disregards distinctions in how candidates represent their positions to voters (e.g., Downs, 1965[1957]; Grofman, 2004). This book builds on studies of positioning by examining how candidate rhetoric surrounding policies affects voter perceptions of those policies. Since this study is among the first to consider how candidates carefully construct their positions as promises or not, I catalog promise and position statements in order to document the distinction between types of statements. For this data, I use statements made by US presidential candidates made in debates from 1960 through 2012, as a sample of visible appeals that cover a wide range of policy spheres, over a wide range of time. The collection of these statements allows me to observe that the distinctions in language exist in practice and not just in theory or the confines of the imagined candidates in experiments.

Second, this work yields empirical evidence that the distinction between promises and positions has ramifications for how voters understand candidates, and that voters notice the distinction between candidates who promise and those who do not. Candidates who make promises polarize voter evaluations based on whether or not voters desire the promised outcome. Because I also find that the rate of promise-making increases over the study period,[7] this finding has implications for our understanding of how rhetoric reflects and reinforces current levels of elite polarization, and potentially for partisan sorting. Voters' attention to the conceptual distinction between promise and non-promise position statements clarifies a reality that voters encounter when they listen to candidate statements, and provides a critical piece of the promissory representation story that has been absent. This book yields important empirical evidence that voters perceive differences between policy statements and that those differences affect understanding of how committed and effective candidates will be on the promised issue. Perhaps more importantly, differences in campaign statements affect whether candidates are more likely to follow through and have the surprising effect of diminishing evaluations of candidate character as well. The work here demonstrates that promises clearly matter to voters and have an important effect on voter evaluations of candidates.

Third, this book demonstrates that the distinction between promises and non-promise policy statements has ramifications for how voters evaluate candidates who have held office. I find that voters differentiate between elected officials who made campaign promises and those who did not. Voters prefer candidates who made a promise and kept it to those who make no promises but more strongly oppose candidates who broke a promise than those who acted out of step with a position on which they never made a promise. Additionally, this data indicates that in some cases, keeping a promise may matter more to voters than the actual position that the candidate took when promising. Both of these findings have important implications for normative theory around representation, accountability, and democracy.

Fourth, this book extends and complements our current understanding of campaign promises, and the ways that campaign promises matter to voters. Currently, much work concludes that candidates keep promises more often than they break them. (I more fully review this literature in Chapter 2, but see Pétry and Collette (2009) and Thomson et al. (2017) for emblematic examples.) Ultimately, there are important distinctions between how institutions and party control can influence which promises are kept and which are broken (Royed, 1996; Artes,

---

[7] This corresponds with other work in the frequency of promises made (Håkansson and Naurin, 2016).

2011; Thomson et al., 2017). However, little attention has been given to understanding how promises matter prospectively, before voters can grapple with the difficulties of fulfillment. One exception shows that voters do have nuanced conceptions of candidates who make promises that alter evaluations at the ballot box (Naurin, 2014). Coupled with Mansbridge (2009), who argues that much of promissory representation relies on the selection of candidates, I argue that attending to the nuances that promises induce on candidate evaluations is a necessary piece of promissory representation, which this book addresses.

Each of these contributions changes how we conceptualize campaigns, voters, and representation. Studies of campaigns need to attend to promises because candidates make them, and they have potential for strategic use. Work centering around how voters interact with campaign information needs to account for the possibility that voters care about promises in a way that can affect their voting behavior in a nuanced manner. Conceptions of representation need to account for the fact that promises matter more than simply highlighting where a candidate stands on the issues. Promises inform voters about candidate commitment and character, and promises cause voters to evaluate candidates differently when considering both future and past actions by candidates.

1.3 EXPLORING THE EFFECT OF CAMPAIGN PROMISES

Ultimately, the theory and evidence that I present in this book shed new light on how promises function and how promises differ from non-promise statements. My research suggests that promises alter voters' perception of a candidate's commitment to an issue, which has implications for a broader understanding of how voters differentiate candidate positions and evaluate candidates.

In this first part of the book, I continue to define promises and distinguish them from other forms of position-taking, as I have in this introduction. In Chapter 2, I develop a theoretical framework to examine how differentiating promises from non-promises might matter to voters. First, I argue that promising increases a candidate's appearance of commitment on an issue. Second, since campaign promises serve as a signal for what candidates will do if elected, by increasing commitment to an issue candidates are sending a stronger signal about their intended actions in office. Because voters tend to hold candidates who act out of step with their policy platforms accountable, they can have relative confidence in a candidate's strong commitment to a position that the latter has promised to enact. It follows then that individuals who hold the same position on the issue will prefer this stronger signal and will more strongly repulse individuals who do not support the candidate's positions. In essence, the result of this argument is that promises should serve to polarize voter opinions of candidates. Because they change perception of commitment to an issue, promises also affect evaluations of potential follow-through and candidate character.

Part II of the book examines whether promises in the real world function as my theory predicts by analyzing both candidates' statements and voters' conceptions of promises. In Chapter 3, I confirm that political candidates commonly make distinctions, examining the first televised presidential election debates, from 1960 and every subsequent set of debates through 2012. While candidates increasingly make both promises and non-promises throughout the period, promises increase at a greater rate than non-promise policy statements. In addition to examining the evidence of this pattern, the chapter suggests that promises are becoming more prevalent among candidates and underscores the utility of considering promises as defined here both in normative theory and in other empirical studies of candidate evaluations.

While real candidates provide plenty of examples of promises and non-promises, it is critical to demonstrate voters' conception of promises as well. While Chapter 3 invoked historical analysis to demonstrate the existence of promises, Chapter 4 introduces survey experiments as the primary means to evaluate voter opinions on promises. These instruments consider how promises on gun control matter to voters. I use gun control as an issue because (1) all types of candidates, over many different election years, have discussed it; (2) voters show strong interest in the issue; and (3) statements around gun control are formulated as promises or non-promises. Chapter 4 also yields evidence that voters agree with the definition of promises given here, and distinguish between promise and non-promise position statements that candidates make. Further, voters anticipate that promises come with elevated expectations of candidate commitment and effectiveness. Part II of the book effectively demonstrates that the proposed definition of promises is ecologically valid through the analyses of candidate statements and voters' responses to them.

In Part III, I turn to the question of the effect of the distinction between promises and non-promises on voter attitudes toward candidates. I demonstrate that promises have important effects on voter evaluations of candidates as well, using experiments to illustrate how promises affect voter support of candidates. In Chapter 5, I demonstrate that promises matter to voters prospectively, and in a nuanced way. Voters who agree with a candidate's statements prefer promisers and those who disagree with a candidate's statement prefer non-promisers. However, promises seem to have a larger negative effect than positive effect that is potentially due to how promises seem to affect candidate evaluations, causing different effects by voter agreement. Respondent expectations for candidate action increase when candidates promise, yet promises also cause assessments of candidate character to become more negative.

In Chapter 6, I further examine the relationship between voter perceptions of candidates and promises by asking how promises affect voters in more nuanced contexts than I describe in Chapter 5. This chapter primarily functions as a robustness check for the data presented in Chapter 5, and includes considering partisan leanings and the number of promises across issues. In Chapter 5, I measure the data using policy cues, but without partisan cues that are a clearly salient element of voter behavior. While promises reinforce partisan lines when politicians make promises that accord with the typical party line, promises slightly advantage candidates who promise against party lines. Next, I examine the question of how promises matter in context of other promises: Specifically, can voters be oversaturated with promises? And if so, do the effects of promises decrease if candidates make more promises? I find that voters view candidates who make promises related to several issues as less likely to act on their promises than those who only make promises related to one issue. However, they still view candidates who promise as more likely than non-promisers to follow through on their action.

Promises make sense as commitments only in that voters hold elected officials accountable for not upholding their commitments (Pitkin, 1967). In Chapter 7, I confirm that distinctions between promises and non-promise position statements matter retrospectively as well. The data in this chapter indicate that voters view candidates who promise and keep their word more favorably than candidates who make no promises. Candidates who promise and break their promises are viewed more negatively than candidates who take the same position without promising. As we might expect, promise-breakers are perceived as less honest and less likely to act in accordance with their word in the future. Additionally, I demonstrate that confidence lost in elected officials who act out of step with their positions is not easily regained. This chapter enhances my overall argument that promises signal commitment because voters do hold candidates accountable, and more stringently so when they promise. Further, it challenges assumptions made by normative theory because it demonstrates that promises matter more to voters than do the actual policy content of the promises.

I conclude in Chapter 8 by discussing the implications of these findings on normative theory and empirical investigations of position-taking and promise-making, and by reflecting on how a nuanced framework of position-taking and promising matters through a discussion of the 2016 presidential election. First, the data here make quite clear that because voters differentiate promises from non-promises, promises polarize voter opinions of candidates. As a result, accounts of candidate evaluations based on positions need to incorporate these distinctions in their work. Theories also must acknowledge voter attitudes toward enforcing democratic institutions verses defining their own positions as well. Second, I argue that empirical investigations into position-taking need to consider the effects of promising (or not) on other important conceptions such as polarization, trust in government, and asymmetries between partisan attitudes. The chapter concludes by illustrating how the argument in this book contributes to many important conversations in political science and future research should build on these findings.

2

Promises as Signals of Commitment

Since Burke (1987) first articulated the differences between trustee and delegate styles of representation, scholars have sought to fully understand how individuals select representatives, and how those processes lead to voter perceptions of representation (Mansbridge, 2009). As cycles of campaigns and elections unfold, it is apparent that the ways in which voters view campaign promises are central to the process of democratic representation as they are responsible for both selecting candidates and assessing elected officials' performances. It is also clear that promises are a critical component of election discussions among the public. For instance, in the United States, prominent news organizations and websites track high-profile candidate promises and the extent to which they keep those promises once in office. Figure 2.1 displays two examples of presidential promises, though PolitiFact tracks several other elected officials as well. During reelection campaigns, incumbents remind constituents of promises kept and challengers remind constituents of promises incumbents have not kept (Benoit, 2000). Indeed, promises and the recall of campaign promises as justification for governance have become more prominent and more critical to political strategy over the last fifty years (Azari, 2014).

In theory as well, promises play a critical role in discussions of representative democracy (Mansbridge, 2003; Thomson et al., 2017). Based on the Mansbridge (2011) definition of promissory representation, promises should matter in two ways. First, prospectively, they should affect the election in which candidates issue campaign pledges and voters select candidates without having seen them act in a particular role as an elected official. Second, promises should also matter retrospectively, as part of

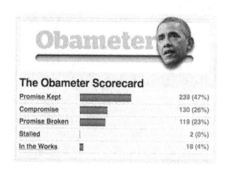

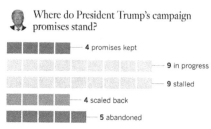

FIGURE 2.1 Examples of promise trackers

These images are screenshots from PolitiFact (Obama) and Los Angeles Times *(Trump), two groups that track promises of elected officials. Several prominent media sources, including* The Washington Post *and* Los Angeles Times, *and CNN conduct their own, similar tallies.*

voters' assessments of elected officials in considering whether to vote for them again. Significant research has considered both of these aspects of the representation pathway, and yet few studies have considered the precise role of the promise itself. To be sure, there is great understanding of how the issue positions that candidates articulate through their promises affect voter decision-making, including what they are, how visible they are, and how important they are. There is also extensive work on how often and what contexts elected officials keep promises. Here, I extend both streams of knowledge by arguing that promises should be considered as a special case of position-taking, both because promises are a critical part of accountability and because they have a nuanced effect on voter evaluations of candidates. Evidence demonstrates that officials typically keep their promises, and we have significant knowledge as to the conditions that support promise-keeping (Naurin, 2014). This work underscores how important promises are to voters as well as illustrates how difficult assessments of promise-keeping are because voters have difficulty ascertaining what it means to keep a promise. My theory builds on Naurin (2014) to extend our knowledge of how promises matter both prospectively and retrospectively because it promotes a slightly different understanding of how voters view promises prospectively and their motivations for assessing promises retrospectively.

This chapter outlines my argument. I explain why promises are a special type of candidate position statement and what candidates might signal by promising on an issue. I begin by discussing why promises merit attention and continue by defining campaign promises. I then show that viewing promises as a strong signal of commitment builds on what we already know about candidate positioning: Promises help candidates address voter concerns about whether or not the former will follow through in favor of the issue stances they take. Finally, I consider how the conceptual distinction between promise and non-promise statements matters retrospectively and give a picture of our current understanding of the fulfillment of campaign promises.

2.1 PROMISSORY REPRESENTATION: A CRITICAL ELEMENT OF REPRESENTATION

Studies of representation often attribute the earliest typology of representation to Burke (1987), who divides it between two types: trustees and delegates. The former are entrusted by the will of the people to use their judgment to represent, while the latter are elected to enact the will of the people. Though Burke's distinction has been adapted and extended to the modern political arena (Mansbridge, 2003, 2011; Rehfeld, 2009; Azari, 2014), a critical next step in clarifying how representation occurs has been to connect representation to accountability mechanisms, which is often inextricably linked to the goals of particular styles of representation. Pitkin (1967) develops a typology of representation that focuses on four distinct types of representation to more clearly assess the meaning of a "good" or successful representative. Formalistic representation (which has evolved into promissory representation) includes both the *authorization* of officials to represent, because they are chosen through legitimate institutions, and the *accountability* of officials to voters, who determine if the official has acted responsibly. Substantive representation invokes how well representatives substitute for their constituents: effectively, how responsive representatives are to the represented individuals (Bühlmann, Widmer, and Schädel, 2010). While both formalistic and substantive representation use an elected official's policy-based actions to assess the job of representation, the final two categories rely on shared identity (often discussed as race, ethnicity, or gender) and valence traits.

Descriptive representation is assessed by how closely representative identities matches population identities, while symbolic representation relies on what symbolism a representative invokes for the represented rather than using shared identity for decision-making. Empirical work has made strides assessing each type of representation, but perhaps accountability is the component that draws the most empirical attention (Mansbridge, 2009). As Pitkin (1967) argues, this may be because, while the standards for judging accountability may vary, it remains the clearest process for assessing how well a representative stands for constituents.

Mansbridge (2003) has offered important modifications to the Pitkin (1967) model, broadening the goals and definitions of descriptive and symbolic representation and substantially clarifying the definition of promissory representation. First, she names promissory representation, incorporating some portions of formalistic representation, in which voters choose candidates because of campaign promises and representatives then "look backward to their promises in acting out the representative relationship" and choosing how to govern (Mansbridge, 2011, p. 627).[1] Second, she broadens descriptive representation into gyroscopic representation. As a part of shared identities or experiences, elected officials have internal compasses that motivate their actions. Third, instead of symbolic representation, she posits surrogate representation, clarifying that voters can feel symbolically represented without having a direct electoral connection to a representative of another community. (For instance, recall Ted Cruz and Beto O'Rourke's Senate race, which drew national attention and for some symbolized a statement for or against Donald Trump (Fernandez, 2018; Borunda and Mekelburg, 2018).) And finally, Mansbridge adds anticipatory representation, a form of representation where a representative acts on issues with the intent to convince voters of their future policy interests rather than responding retrospectively.[2] Most relevant to the discussion here, the promissory representation model features candidates who specify policy stances and voters who elect candidates to carry out those platforms – as in

---

[1] Dovi (2018) says that promissory representation most closely resembles formalistic representation.

[2] Rehfeld (2009) and Mansbridge (2011) have further debated the merits of the Mansbridge (2003) categories, largely focusing on how to better interpret realized aspects of trustee and mandate models of representation within gyroscopic representation, the Mansbridge (2003) version of descriptive representation. Since this book focuses on promissory representation, and the selection process based on issues, I ignore the contributions of that discussion here.

a principal–agent model. While promissory representation is only one conception of representation, as Mansbridge (2003) describes, it is "one of the most important ways in which citizens influence political outcomes through their representatives" (p. 516), and it remains one of the most highly studied conceptions of representation.

Miller and Stokes (1963) propose two stages to the process that ensures promissory representation: the selection pathway (or voting) and the sanction pathway (how voters choose to reward or punish the actions of elected officials in office and bids for reelection). Initially, research focused on the second pathway, conceptualizing how voters sanctioned candidates and how the fear of sanctioning pre-committed candidates during the selection portion of the process, However, both theoretical and empirical evidence suggest that the sanction model does not do the work that it anticipated (Mansbridge, 2009). Under the sanction model, voters can sanction candidates who break faith with them by acting out of step with campaign pledges by withdrawing support, and this possibility causes candidates to commit to specific actions within their campaigns (Aragones, Postlewaite, and Palfrey, 2007). Researchers often empirically describe support for incumbents in terms of a change in votes or campaign funding (Grossman and Helpman, 2005; Alston and Mueller, 2006; Mayhew, 2004[1974]; Fiorina, 1974; Baron, 1989). However, the selection pathway seems to dominate the process of voter decision-making and, perhaps more importantly, sanctioning mechanisms are not always supported by empirical evidence (Bianco, 1994). Further, instead of sanctioning officials in subsequent elections, voters appear to use the additional information as a secondary type of selection mechanism, namely, as security evidence to support officials who are more likely to follow through on their word over actors who have gone back on promises (Fearon, 1999). Thus, future campaign promises of incumbents who have kept their word are more compelling if accompanied by evidence of previously fulfilled promises (Elinder, Jordahl, and Poutvaara, 2015).

Attempts to understand voters' selection mechanisms focus on how candidates' issue positions influence election outcomes. At the root of much of this literature is the Downsian proposal of the median voter, which argues that voters seek policy outcomes by choosing candidates whose policy platforms align with theirs, and candidates choose policy outcomes to align with voters (Downs, 1965[1957]). This is known as proximity voting. As Mayhew (2004[1974]) notes, candidate position-taking is one of the most important aspects of a candidate's goal toward winning elections. Much effort has concentrated on how specifically this pathway operates. While some have followed Downs in arguing for proximity voting, others have developed theories of how voters might align with candidates based on issues that require a more nuanced understanding of both the issues as well as the policy space.[3] Grofman (1985) proposes that voters use candidate positions to estimate how the status quo will change if the candidate wins, noting that some positions may not be realized. In this conception, voters *discount* candidates whose projected polices may not be realized or whose policies may be thought to move the status quo closest to voter preferences. In a third version of how position-taking matters, Rabinowitz and Macdonald (1989) propose that voters directionally select candidates so that they prefer candidates on their side of the issue, and of candidates on their side of the issue, they prefer the most extreme candidates available. Experimental evidence testing between these types of voting behavior suggests that proximity voting is the most common method of candidate selection (as well as the theory most discussed in the literature), and it is clear that candidate positions have a strong influence on vote choice and that all iterations of selection based on positions are present among voters (Tomz and Houweling, 2008).

Another stream of research examines whether variations in how issue positions are stated could potentially matter to voters, and in particular the degree of specificity with which candidates detail their positions. For instance, candidates may benefit from obscuring their precise position on an issue if they are uncertain about positions in their constituency (Shepsle, 1972; Page, 1976). Likewise, they may choose to obscure their true positions as a way to build their voting base even if they are certain about constituent positions (Alesina and Cukierman, 1990; Glazer, 1990; Meirowitz, 2005). Despite arguments that voters dislike ambiguity, evidence suggests broad, less precise statements do not necessarily alienate them (Tomz and Houweling, 2009). Lindgren and Naurin (2017) found that ambiguity used in candidate position descriptions can sway voters, primarily moderate ones, in their favor. Beside presentation of candidate positions, other factors can affect how voters filter issue positions. These include the importance of an issue to voters, similarity between candidates' ideas and those of their opponents, and even valence issues,

---

[3] Grofman (2004) offers a useful review of these, nicely categorized by the assumptions that Downs (1965[1957]) makes.

such as character or personality. (See Krosnick, Visser, and Harder (2010) for a review.)

To date, investigations into various aspects of the selection mechanisms have examined one aspect of promissory representation: how voters use positions to make decisions. These studies underscore the centrality and significance of candidate issue-positioning to voter selection of elected officials and our understanding of promissory representation in democratic models. However, the feature of promises in the promissory representation is somewhat lost within this field of knowledge, as it tends to treat candidate positioning as unidimensional, looking only at the binary question as to whether the candidates declare a position on a topic and failing to take into account differences between promises and non-promise positions. Thus, it assumes voters judge all policy statements primarily on the content of the issues expressed and ignores the degree to which the statement is viewed as a promise.

Research *has* investigated the importance of promises, however. Indeed, promises are central to a wealth of literature seeking to understand the mandate portion of promissory representation and candidate attentiveness to accountability. In addition to showing that elected officials act on most of the promises they make in office (Naurin, 2002, 2014; Thomson, 2001; Artes, 2011; Kostadinova, 2013; Naurin, 2014; Thomson et al., 2017), this literature shows that variations in the types of promise exist and may interact with other features to alter how voters view fulfilled promises (e.g., Elinder, Jordahl, and Poutvaara, 2015). For instance, Royed (1996) investigates what she refers to as the hardness of promises (firm commitments compared to soft commitments) and the specificity of promises. She finds little correlation between hardness and specificity of promises and the success with which politicians keep promises. However, Thomson (2001) demonstrates the hardness of the promise varies by country context, with more variation occurring in the United Kingdom and United States. Yet investigations tend to group the types of promise (including hardness and specificity) together in demonstrating high levels of promise-keeping in government-controlled parties and lower amounts of promise-keeping in opposition parties (e.g., Thomson, 2001; Mansergh and Thomson, 2007). Importantly, Mansergh and Thomson (2007) illustrate variation in how well the mandate model works across country contexts, which adds evidence to the notion that the external motivation of elected officials keeping promises (Fox and Rothenberg, 2011) is not certain, and elected officials may be internally motivated to keep their promises (Sulkin, 2009). Regardless of why

elected officials keep promises, they do more often than not, emphasizing the importance of promises in democratic discourse. Moreover,
promises have become more frequent in national party language than
in the past (Håkansson and Naurin, 2016; Thomson et al., 2017).
Specifically within the United States, candidates have increasingly used
mandate claims and language invoking campaign promises to justify,
celebrate, and claim credit since the 1960s (Azari, 2014). Clearly, the
work centering on promises emphasizes the centrality of promises to
representation as it considers the ways in which promise fulfillment
occurs and matters to voters.

   Whether voters see promises and candidates who make them differently remains to be determined. Since candidates' stances on issues affect
voters differently depending on the issue (Slothuus and De Vreese, 2010),
it makes sense to believe that voters would also be more responsive to
issues on which candidates have made promises. It likewise makes sense
to investigate how promises matter to voters in and of themselves – do
projections of a higher level of commitment change voter perceptions of
those candidates? Evidence shows that the particular linguistic content
of position statements affects voter evaluations (Lindgren and Naurin,
2017)[4] and the way in which voters weigh future promises against fulfilled promises (Elinder, Jordahl, and Poutvaara, 2015). Naurin (2011)
illustrates how voters view promise-keeping as a unique form of position-
taking and the differential role position statements play in their decision-
making. Given candidate selection is clearly one of the most important
aspects of promissory representation and promissory representation has
long dominated discussions of how voters are represented, the effect of
promises on voter behavior is an essential investigation. Further, the investigation matters even more if promises elevate the amount of commitment
candidates indicate on issues. Mayhew (2004[1974]) argues

"that politicians often get rewarded for taking positions rather than achieving
effects.... It may look good back home to favor "gun control" or "saving Social
Security" even though laws bearing those labels might not amount to much"
(p. xv).

---

[4] Here, the authors investigate the use of persuasive language, employed through more
descriptive adjectives, and find that voters find the elevated use of adjectives appealing.
While this study more closely investigates components of ambiguity and specificity than
the use of promises and commitment, it underscores that voters do use more than a
position statement to make their decisions.

If candidates are rewarded for the positions themselves, then certainly they would be rewarded for the appearance of commitment to the issues as well.

2.2 ASSESSING REPRESENTATION AND CAMPAIGN PROMISES

Definitions of promises vary widely across studies of representation (Pétry and Collette, 2009), and there is no formal mechanism of enforcement for promises.[5] Those studies employing a clear operational definition of campaign promises can either use quite broad definitions or not provide an operational definition of what it means to promise, identifying promises from a set of platforms or speeches without a decision rule on what constitutes a promise or not, often determining any position to be a promise. For instance, Fishel (1985) and Krukones (1984) both provide instructive studies of American presidents throughout the twentieth century, demonstrating that US presidents typically follow through on their promises.[6] Such studies might include any policy appeal, regardless of whether fulfillment is feasible or not (Aragones, Postlewaite, and Palfrey, 2007; Sulkin, 2009). Or, despite more specific decision rules, studies use broad proxies. While these decisions make sense for studies of fulfillment, they do not differentiate between varied levels of commitment. For instance, Ringquist and Dasse (2004) measure promises by observing support for various policies assessed by the National Political Awareness Test, a survey where candidates indicate support or opposition on a variety of positions rather than using organic campaign speech where specificity and commitment may vary.[7]

For this study, I propose a definition of promising that distinguishes promises as a specific form of position-taking. Here, I refer to campaign promise as a position statement where the candidate attaches an expectation of action the candidate will perform in office or an outcome that

---

5 As Manin (1997) describes, formal mechanisms did exist in England until the eighteenth century, because conceptions of representation reflected a legal requirement for candidates to follow through on campaign pledges.

6 For further examples refer to Pétry and Collette (2009), a meta-analysis of studies on promises that gives other examples, including Bradley (1969) and Rallings (1987).

7 The authors acknowledge the operational definition of promise here is not an ideal way to identify promises, further underlining the difficulty of measuring campaign promises. That said, the authors are consistent with the perspective that promises are a way to indicate commitment by assuming that surveyed support acts as a likely indicator of candidate intent to perform an action when in office.

will be achieved if that candidate is elected.[8] This could include any policy action a candidate could take in office: proposing or voting for a bill or signing an executive order.[9] For example, a candidate could state "I promise that I will not increase taxes" or "When I am in the White House, I will not increase taxes." Both would constitute promises. Likewise, for this study I consider a promise of inaction, or a promise not to do something or to preserve the status quo, is just as much of a promise as a promise to do something. However, I add to previous research by further investigating promises against non-promise position statements, which are statements that reveal the candidate's stance on an issue without giving any expectation of action if elected. For instance, a candidate who says "I am in favor of providing affordable health care" is not making a promise.

The proposed definition of a promise is consistent with colloquial use: Merriam-Webster (2014) defines a promise as "a statement telling someone that you will definitely do something or that something will definitely happen in the future." This definition is also consistent with other conceptual definitions of promise-making. Mayhew (2004[1974]) underlines this distinction by pointing to the possibility of explicit and implicit positions. In studies examining the rates of promise fulfillment, scholars often offer a distinctive definition of promise-making, typically emphasizing a candidate's declaration of action upon election (Naurin, 2014). Royed (1996) defines promising as "a commitment to carry out some action or produce some outcome," and also distinguishes between hard promises, where a candidate links herself to a policy action, and soft promises, where a candidate only expresses agreement with an action. Thus, Royed makes the same distinction I do but does not explore the implications of the distinction and its effects on prospective decision-making. Subsequent work also points out variation within promises, but tends to highlight

---

[8] In accordance with this definition, Druckman, Kifer, and Parkin (2009) find that candidates strongly prefer to make action statements over taking positions. My argument here attempts to explain that observation.

[9] Expected outcomes can also be voiced by politicians in terms of actual outcomes as well, such as lowering taxes or decreasing unemployment. Royed (1996) and Naurin (2014) discuss these distinctions more directly. In the data section, I test only promises voiced as commitment to act in accordance with a principle. There may be distinctions in how voters treat promises of action or outcomes.

the criteria for observable promise fulfillment as markers of promises themselves rather than distinctions between how promises are made.[10]

Finally, Royed (1996) uses a more narrow approach than I do, requiring that a promise have an explicit degree of commitment, or a performative utterance, incorporated into the statement, such as "I promise," "I pledge," or even "I support" or "I agree."[11] These statements help to distinguish between a promise and a non-promise position, but excluding them removes one of the most famous commitments made (and broken) in the US context: when George H. W. Bush said at the Republican National Convention in 1988, "My opponent won't rule out raising taxes. But I will. And the Congress will push me to raise taxes, and I'll say no, and they'll push, and I'll say no, and they'll push again, and I'll say, to them, 'Read my lips: no new taxes' " (Bush, 1988). The action is clear: He would not allow new taxes to be enacted on his watch, and the public reading of this statement as a strong promise, both prospectively and retrospectively, also supports this definitional consideration. More importantly, this statement is routinely viewed as a promised commitment to voters in the 1988 election cycle.

The distinction between promised and non-promised position statements importantly is not a difference of specificity in the actual position itself, rather a distinction in whether the candidate specifies an action or an outcome. This difference is important because it distinguishes this theory from other theories that conceptualize candidate ambiguity. The theory of candidate ambiguity is that by making issue positions more or less clear to voters, candidates alter voter evaluations. Several studies suggest that candidates increase their vote share by taking ambiguous stands on policy issues, effectively obscuring differences between themselves and voters, thus appealing to a wider range of voters (Shepsle, 1972; Page, 1978, 1976). Some posit that ambiguity does not

---

[10] Royed (1996), Royed and Borrelli (1997, 1999), Naurin (2002, 2014), and Artes (2011) all focus on a broad approach to fulfillment such that their definition of promises does not require candidates to provide criteria to assess the success of the statement in order to be considered a promise. Thomson (2001), Kostadinova (2013, 2015), and Thomson et al. (2017) use a more narrow definition of promise fulfillment, requiring candidate promises to incorporate criteria. I do not focus on that particular distinction between testable and non-testable statements as I am not concerned with what it means to keep a promise and instead focus on the differences in voters' perception between when candidates make promises and when they do not.

[11] This can be a point of disagreement within this line of work as well. Thomson (2001) notes these "harder" statements are much more common in certain country contexts.

increase the number of votes for candidates (Campbell, 1983; Berinsky and Lewis, 2007), while other studies argue that ambiguity results in voter uncertainty about their own policy positions or those of candidates and thus decreases support of ambiguous candidates (Bartels, 1986; Alvarez, 1997; Brady and Ansolabehere, 1989; Callander and Wilson, 2008). More recently, experiments indicate that deploying ambiguity seems to be a more rewarding strategy than delivering clearer indications of positions to voters (Tomz and Houweling, 2009). And in general, candidates seem to be more willing to obfuscate their position than to clearly state their position. The rhetorical strategy of promising may seem similar to ambiguity because a candidate might seem to give more information to voters about a position if they promise, but that is not necessarily the case. A promise elicits information about action on an issue which differs from ambiguity, a concept that refers to how candidates may disclose or obscure different components of their positions. For instance, a candidate could take a stance on whether raising taxes is a good idea or not. That candidate could be less ambiguous by highlighting which income groups should have taxes raised or lowered. The candidate could talk about why any of these stances is a good idea without promising, or could promise to implement policy in line with their stance.

2.3 PROMISES AS SIGNALS OF COMMITMENT

As Mansbridge (2003) details, the basic model of promissory representation is a principal-agent relationship between voters (principals) and politicians (agents), where the voters' power comes from the ability to vote uncooperative agents out of office. Voters then are faced with a commitment problem: Elected officials may face incentives to make a promise prior to elections but a different set of incentives to act on policy as an elected official (Grossman and Helpman, 2005). Candidate positions have long been viewed as signals of candidate intentions in office to voters (Downs, 1965[1957]; Austen-Smith and Banks, 1989), and the signals can be about how they will act as well as what type of elected officials they may be. For instance, candidates can use positions to signal how they will act or as a way to pander to voters. When models account for elected officials' potential to break promises or even lie about positions, they illustrate concepts of two-party divergence and polarization (Grofman, 2004). Positions can signal something about candidate character as well. By allowing for uncertainty in whether candidates are honest and whether they engage in cheap talk, models demonstrate that dishonest candidates can have an advantage because voters are forced to rely on idealized conceptions of position statements rather than act on whether candidates will actually follow through on those positions (Callander and Wilkie, 2007). Huang (2010) points out that this implies that lying candidates only succeed in an environment where the norm is for candidates to honor their positions.

Ultimately, candidates can engage in strategy around the types of positions they take, by their intent to follow through on them, or by potentially changing valence (Callander, 2008*b*). Voter judgments are fraught with uncertainty about both the platforms the candidates are presenting and whether candidates will follow through on their platforms after they have been elected (Kartik and McAfee, 2007). What remains unanswered in these models is how candidates signal their type to voters, and whether signals of varying commitment affect voter judgments of candidates.

Given that candidates can choose whether or not to make a promise when they take a position, what might incentivize candidates to promise? Generally speaking, there is a lot of uncertainty in elections. There is uncertainty about what policies voters want (Converse, 1964; Zaller, 1992), what voters think candidates support (Bartels, 1986, 1988; Alvarez and Franklin, 1994; Vavreck, 1997; Alvarez, 1997), and whether candidates will actually act as they say they will (Naurin, 2014). Despite the fact that most candidates keep more than half of their promises, average American citizens expect candidates to break their promises regularly (Pétry and Collette, 2009; Naurin, 2011). Candidates have incentive to reduce the amount of uncertainty about whether they will act on an issue or not.[12] The way that promises affect voters, however, depends on whether voters alter their expectations for candidate action or change opinions about the candidate's character traits because of them.

2.3.1 Position-Taking and the Nuances of Promises

The underlying assumption to be tested here is that promises send stronger signals of commitment to voters, and how we might anticipate voters may react in response. First, a signal of greater commitment could

---

[12] As described above, the theory of ambiguity argues both sides of a similar coin. Candidates may lose attractiveness to some voters by being more clear about their policy positions, while they may gain some supporters by being more specific. Tomz and Houweling (2009) demonstrate that, in most cases, candidates do better by being ambiguous. Again, it is important to emphasize that promises are not necessarily about being specific about where the candidate lies on policy but about being more specific about *if* the candidate intends to do something about the policy.

mean that candidates potentially could shift voter understanding about how the candidate will work toward realizing that policy stance, thereby altering a voter's interpretation of how policy in that space might shift as a result of election. In determining a candidate's position, voters face an important problem. Candidate positions can be obscured by uncertainty both in information voters have about the candidates and whether the candidates will follow through on those platforms (Callander, 2008a). As Alvarez (1997) argues, "An important determinant of voter information levels is the context of the campaign.... In other words, what voters know or don't know of the candidates and the policy issues in any election is largely determined by the information and the clarity of that information, presented to them during the presidential campaign" (p. 25). Promises however, might allow for candidates to help solve both problems. A signal of strong commitment could help clarify to the voters that the candidate is more likely to act on that particular policy. Promises might also increase a voter's attention to the issue as the candidate is signaling to voters the importance of the issue and thereby reducing uncertainty around their stance on the issue. In so doing, candidates might strategically manipulate their promises to highlight aspects of their agenda, which is an oft-cited goal of policy platforms.

In everyday discourse, people can reduce uncertainty about whether they will adhere to their commitments by erecting mechanisms that will impose costs on them if they do not – specifically, costs higher than those they will incur if they do keep their commitments (Charness and Dufwenberg, 2006, 2010). Promises induce a positive effect when kept and a much larger negative effect when broken (Buehler, Griffin, and Ross, 1994; Robinson and Rousseau, 1994; Gneezy and Epley, 2014). While voters do not clearly sanction candidates who do not perform as they pledge, they do express frustration and disappointment when candidates do not follow through (Rousseau, 1995; Naurin, 2014). Thus, promise-making may be one important way that candidates can assure voters of their intentions on a policy because they are building an inherently costly checkpoint for voters if, as elected officials, they do not act on the specific issue. Because voters prefer candidates who align with their views, promises should reinforce preferences for candidates with similar views. Promises should also reinforce dislike for candidates whose positions are dissimilar.

Research has confirmed that messages affect voter behavior in several important ways. Vavreck (2009) demonstrates that the content of the message strongly influences voters. She demonstrates that when the economy has been good, presidential candidates from the current party in office perform best when discussing the economy and challengers perform best when focusing on a different set of issues. In contrast, when the economy has been bad, challengers should focus on the economy and incumbents should focus on a different set of issues. Here, I consider an additional way in which candidate rhetoric may be strategic: by altering perceived levels of commitment. Candidates use their past records (whether for reelection to the same position, election to a new position, or nongovernmental experience for novices to governance) to assure voters about their intentions in upcoming elections (Burden, 2007; Hall, 1996; Koger, 2003; Sellers, 1998; Schiller, 1995; Sulkin, 2009, 2005; Sides, 2006). Whether candidates do so because they themselves have acted on policy issues or because their party is seen as more competent on that issue, past records may help assuage doubts that the candidate is simply embracing a position to attract votes, and not because the candidate will act on that position in the future. Promises may be an alternative tool through which candidates may assure voters of their intents in office. And, even if voters follow party leaders in deciding how to care about issues (Lenz, 2013; Adams, Ezrow, and Somer-Topcu, 2011, 2014), talking about issues in particular ways has the potential to change how voters understand those issues and how strongly they support party leadership on those issues.

A voter's evaluation of a promise would be based on the voter's alignment with the position the candidate takes. Say that a candidate takes a position (C) on an issue, where the current policy is SQ, or the status quo (pictured in Figure 2.2). A promised statement (P) should both increase the perceived commitment that a candidate makes and decrease the uncertainty about whether the candidate will act on the issue at all, resulting in a higher possibility of shifting policy closer to the candidate's stated position and the voter's preference. A non-promise statement then could signal a smaller chance of the status quo shifting toward the candidate's position because the candidate might possibly do nothing about that position. As a result, voters' position on the issue would affect their judgment of the candidates. Voters strongly preferring the promised action (V_2 in Figure 2.2) would strongly prefer the promiser because they would perceive the candidate as more committed to that position and, thus, more likely to implement the policy the voters favor. On the other hand, voters on the other side of the issue spectrum (V_1 in Figure 2.2) would prefer a candidate who did not promise on the issue position. They would perceive a candidate who did not promise as less committed to the issue and less likely to follow

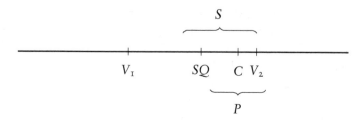

FIGURE 2.2 How voters perceive policy statements

The line represents the essence of viewing promises as commitments. For a candidate's policy position, centered at C, a candidate can choose to make a promise, P, or a non-promise, S. V_1 and V_2 represent two different voters in the candidate's district.

through on it and, thus, less likely to move the position from the status quo to further away from the voter's ideal point.

2.3.2 Promises and Candidate Character

The second way that promising might affect voter evaluations of candidates is by changing perceptions of valence. Stokes (1963) initially conceived of valence as potential rewards to candidates. In part, these considerations were termed valence because there is general consensus about the desired outcomes (Stokes, 1966). This literature generally focuses on candidate character, and I consider it here as others have (Kartik and McAfee, 2007). Kinder et al. (1980) describe an ideal president as "politically trustworthy," "honest and open-minded" (p. 320). As this literature has evolved, scholars have identified four character traits that affect voter evaluations of presidents: competence, leadership, integrity, and empathy or open-mindedness (Funk, 1999; Kinder et al., 1980; Goren, 2007, 1997).

When candidate positions are held equal, research tells us that better valence ratings give candidates an advantage in voter evaluations (Groseclose, 2001; Miller and Stokes, 1963; Kinder, 1986). Candidate positions can be used to increase perceptions of character, integrity in particular (Kartik and McAfee, 2007). Additionally, candidates combine issue appeals with those on character to further boost evaluations (Just, 1996; Kern, 1989). Promise-making could be such a case, where candidates use a specific rhetorical strategy to remind voters of positive character traits. Indeed, "trait images are increasingly recognized as tightly interconnected with issue positions" (Funk, 1999, p. 700). (See also Green (2007); Jacobs and Shapiro (1994); Kaid and Chanslor (1995).)

Like other studies of strategic promises, this study focuses on how candidates might alter perceptions of integrity, which I measure with honesty, or empathy, which I measure with open-mindedness. Because promising is less likely to have a direct effect on perceptions of competence or leadership, until the outcome of the commitment is revealed (Funk, 1996), I ignore those two aspects of candidate character here. I hypothesize that a promise might signal honesty to a voter, since it suggests the candidate is willing to reveal future actions. This is consistent with signaling theories that candidates have incentive to be honest, because too much dishonesty produces harsher electoral environments (Callander and Wilkie, 2007). Increasing perceptions of candidate character should then also improve a candidate's overall appeal to voters (Grose and Husser, 2014). While it is possible that voters will conceive of candidate character holistically, such that ratings of honesty and open-mindedness move together, it is possible that ratings of open-mindedness are considered differently. Candidates who promise may also be perceived as less willing to empathize with others or change their minds. Unlike expectations of candidate action, which are dependent upon candidate–voter position alignment, promises should have a relatively similar effect on voter assessments of candidate character regardless of candidate position. Because of projection, where voters attach more positive effect to candidates with similar positions, promises might yield slightly higher character ratings between candidates and parties who agree (Krosnick, 1990), but on the whole I anticipate that it should be quite minimal.

2.3.3 Other Possible Effects of Promises

Figure 2.3 summarizes my expectations about how promises affect voters. Note that the effect of promising is moderated by agreement in the pathway about commitments and expectations of follow-through but not for candidate traits. Public opinion data notes voter distrust, both in the government to do what is right and of candidates to follow through on their promises, makes it possible for promises to have an alternative effect on voter evaluations of candidates. Voters are notoriously skeptical of what they consider pandering: empty candidate rhetoric focused on getting votes rather than changing policy (Canes-Wrone, Herron, and Shotts, 2001; Jacobs and Shapiro, 2000).

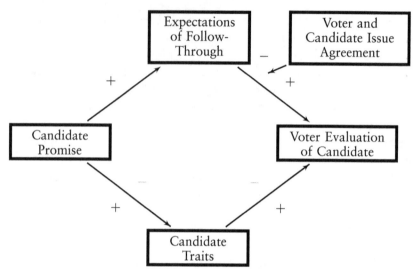

FIGURE 2.3 Theorized effect of promises

This pathway summarizes how promises might affect voter evaluations of candidates. The black signs are the pathway described in Sections 2.3.1 (upper path) and Section 2.3.2 (lower path), while the gray signs are the alternatives discussed in Section 2.3.3.

As a result, if voters connect promises to pandering rather than an actual interest in the policy, promises may in fact induce negative judgments for expectations of follow-through, regardless of candidate commitment (McGraw, Lodge, and Jones, 2002).

Similarly, promising may negatively impact how a voter perceives a candidate's character. I anticipate that ratings of open-mindedness will decrease with promises, but impressions of honesty may decrease as well. As with expectations of follow-through, promising may make the candidate seem less honest because it may be considered posturing on a position simply to pander to voters. If this is true, voters should universally prefer a non-promising candidate. Voters sharing the same position would prefer the non-promiser because she is more honest and not posturing. Voters taking a different position may prefer the non-promiser because she is also more honest. For this potential alternative, I have no expectation that voter–candidate agreement on an issue will moderate either pathway, or that promises will have an exclusively negative effect on candidate evaluations.

2.3.4 Promises in Context of Campaigns

While the general pathway outlined above is the backbone of my argument, I have not yet considered other contextual effects of elections. The possibilities for enriching the context of my theory are endless, but I focus here on two additional considerations. First, how do promises matter in context of partisan information (cued not simply by the actual position)? Second, how do they matter in the context of other issues?

With respect to the first question, research shows parties in power tend to increase the rate of promise fulfillment more than parties out of power (Mansergh and Thomson, 2007; Artes, 2011; Thomson et al., 2017). In the context of partisan information, I examine how promises affect partisan attachment as well as alignment of issues. Due to the partisan nature of today's political systems, it is possible that co-partisans receive promises best, regardless of the issue position. Essentially, co-partisans may project the beneficial aspects of promising onto the candidates despite the position taken (Krosnick, 1990).

Further, the issue ownership literature suggests candidates use issues and records to highlight their relative strengths (Petrocik, 1996). And, often, the most persuasive issues are those that align with one's own party. As argued in this literature and elsewhere, candidates and parties build reputations for themselves on particular issues (Rabinowitz and Macdonald, 1989). It is to a candidate's advantage then to repeatedly highlight these issues, particularly when voters are most concerned about them (Ansolabehere and Iyengar, 1994). If parties tend to "own" issues, it is likely that candidates can more successfully promise on particular issues based on their party. Among voters, candidates perform best when they advertise on party-specific issues (Ansolabehere and Iyengar, 1994). Over time, ownership has been demonstrated through other surveys of public opinion as well as candidate speech analysis (Petrocik, 1996; Petrocik, Benoit, and Hansen, 2003; Brazeal and Benoit, 2001; Jarvis, 2004; Shaw, 1998). It follows that Democrats promise more on "Democratic" issues and Republicans promise more on "Republican" issues. However, candidates who can demonstrate a record that is contrary to their party's general position may break these patterns (Brazeal and Benoit, 2001). Thus, it is entirely possible that candidates gain from promising on an issue across party lines because they are elevating their perceived commitment on the issue regardless of partisanship.

With respect to the question of how promises matter in the context of the discussion of other issues, consider that while candidates prefer to focus on a particular subset of issues (Krosnick, 1988), it would be a rare candidate who does not attend to a multitude of issues. While making promises has both positive and negative effects, I argue that as candidates makes more promises, the potential benefit of promising decreases.

If promises increase a candidate's commitment to an issue, a greater number of promises should signal overcommitment and put into question a candidate's relative commitment to each issue. Candidates can surely commit to action on more than one policy position, but the weight the commitment carries should decrease once a certain number of promises are made. If promising indicates that a candidate will be more likely to act, or finds an issue more important than other issues, the effects of promising will become meaningless if the candidate makes too many promises and oversaturates the electorate with promises. In particular, a candidate has a finite number of resources, time, and energy, and could not possibly make a promise on every issue. More specifically, making several promises may cause voters to doubt how serious the candidate is about actually investing effort in that issue. If candidates are trying to signal a clearer issue position, they also might signal that they are less likely to realize that issue position because they have so many goals at hand. Or, if the candidate is trying to signal issue importance, increasing the number of issues that are important would decrease the relative importance of each issue. Thus, the more promises a candidate makes on different issues, the less expectations voters should have that the candidate will act on each of them.

2.4 COMMITMENT, PROMISE FULFILLMENT, AND RETROSPECTIVE JUDGMENTS

In its purest form, the selection model considers an election cycle as a single face-off between candidates and voters (Mansbridge, 2009). In reality, as long as candidates are not limited to a single term, elections tend to be a repeated game, and candidates think about future elections, including by shaping campaign strategies with future outcomes in mind (Aragones, Postlewaite, and Palfrey, 2007; Callander, 2008b). If promises send a strong signal about potential candidate action in office prospectively, they should also have an important retrospective effect on judgments of candidates as well because promise fulfillment or breaking signals to voters which type the elected official is (Fearon, 1999).

One of the most difficult questions facing those studying representation is how to appropriately measure candidate accountability and responsiveness (Dovi, 2012). Literature strongly underscores the notion that voters view elected officials who do not keep promises negatively, but since most of these studies consider promises retrospectively, they tend to focus on how many promises are fulfilled and the conditions under which those promises are fulfilled rather than what incentive candidates have to fulfill promises. I argue that since candidates who promise during the campaign make a more significant commitment to a position, not following through on that position should be more costly for candidates who promise than those who take the same position and yet do not follow through on the initial campaign position.

2.4.1 Promise Fulfillment

Studies of campaign promises have concentrated largely on the rate of fulfillment, but several observations about when we might expect promises to occur and the frequency nonetheless emerge. First, candidates tend to keep the promises that they make while campaigning. Early studies of presidential promises in the United States illustrate this by matching statements in convention speeches to actions in office that contradicted expectations.[13] Krukones (1984) points out that campaigns are filled with distortion, falsehood, irrelevancy, ambiguity, and evasion, but finds that presidents from Wilson through Reagan kept three-fourths of their promises. Fishel (1985) confirmed these results, comparing party platforms to presidential follow-through from 1958 through 1984. Sulkin (2011) similarly finds that among congressional candidates, attention to issues effectively predicts their attention to policy action once in office, suggesting that this tendency to enact campaign promises holds true regardless of office.

Additionally, much analysis of European party pledges has demonstrated that officials fulfill the bulk of pledges their parties make, from Sweden to Spain to the United Kingdom. Government styles (multiparty versus two-party as in Royed (1996)) affect these patterns, and parties in power are more likely to keep their promises (Artes, 2011). (Though Kostadinova (2013) finds whether a party is in power has no impact

---

[13] The Burkean version of democracy envisions representatives as unconstrained (Manin, 1997).

in Bulgaria.) Pétry and Collette (2009), who perform a meta-analysis of the findings of many of these studies, estimate that, in aggregate, candidates keep 67% of their promises. However, Pétry and Collette (2009) ignore whether the original studies investigated single candidates or party platforms as well as the branch of government in which the elected officials were running.

An important empirical puzzle emerges with regard to how voters perceive the likelihood that politicians and parties will fulfill their promises. Evidence spanning decades and continents shows candidate commitment to fulfilling their pledges. Yet, voters overwhelmingly expect candidates to break promises if elected both in Europe and the United States (Sulkin, 2011). Naurin (2014) dubs this the *pledge paradox* and uses interviews of voters to illustrate that the disbelief stems from voter interpretation of a narrative about democracy and politicians rather than real examples, as well as mismatches between how voters, politicians, and researchers determine what constitutes a fulfilled promise. While Naurin (2014) focuses on the question as to why voters believe this against the evidence that elected officials keep their promises, demonstrating that voters have complex views of what promise fulfillment may mean. In particular, voters sometimes define promises differently than scholars and, in other cases, attribute their own policy preferences on what elected officials *should have promised* rather than what was actually promised.

Some researchers propose that candidates have an internal motivation to take stances and act on them. Sulkin (2011) stipulates this as the core of her theory; most candidates are motivated by principles, and they take positions they wholeheartedly embrace. As a result, candidates who follow through on their promises are simply pursuing policies they believe in. Coupling past interest, records, and campaign statements with attention to issues when in office, Sulkin (2011) effectively demonstrates that candidates do have some measure of internal motivation to keep their promises.

They also have an external motivation. Even if sanctioning is not the most important avenue in defining representation, prospective strategies still leave room for retrospective considerations by voters. (See Banks (1990), Harrington (1993), and Aragones, Postlewaite, and Palfrey (2007).) Whether the pathway is construed as one of sanctioning or updated signaling–as Fearon (1999) argues–voters can reject the reelection of officials who break promises or change positions in subsequent elections by not supporting incumbents or decreasing campaign contributions (Grossman and Helpman, 2005; Alston and Mueller, 2006;

Mayhew, 2004[1974]; Fiorina, 1974; Baron, 1989). This literature also suggests that part of the incumbent advantage stems from having kept promises, which signal that the candidate will make credible future commitment as well (McGillivray, 1997; Grossman and Helpman, 2005; Alston and Mueller, 2006; Sulkin, 2005). And the possibility of forfeiting reelection in subsequent elections induces candidates to commit to actions in their campaigns (Aragones, Postlewaite, and Palfrey, 2007).

2.4.2 The Lasting Commitment Implied by Promises

Adding to our knowledge of how voters view promises, I focus on a different aspect of what promises mean to voters beyond fulfillment. Specifically, because I ask what role promises have for voters in the prospective pathway, I also am interested in understanding the long-term effects these promises would have in subsequent election terms. What benefit do candidates have from making promises (and continuing to make even more promises) if voters are skeptical of candidate promises? Importantly, this acts as a further test of whether promises increase perceptions of commitment to issues. If voters use prospective position-taking in any capacity to evaluate elected officials, then does changing the imbued level of commitment also change how voters evaluate promises as kept and effect subsequent evaluations?

That increasing commitment to an issue and breaking with that commitment yields stronger judgments by voters is demonstrated by how negatively voters view candidates who act against signed pledges, such that Tomz and Van Houweling (2012b) predict that candidates will only break their pledges if nearly all constituents disagree with the pledge. I fully expect to see a similar negative cost to breaking a promise. Because promises should be perceived as higher levels of commitment, I anticipate that broken promises will be more costly to candidates than acting out of step with a non-promise position. As Fenno (2004[1973]) argues, congressional officials must spend much of their time defending their votes and the incentive to act in a manner not advertised has a large potential cost to reelection. Thus, the signal of increased commitment should make breaking a promise more costly for elected officials than acting out of step with a non-promised position. Even if voters do not remember a promise a candidate made during an election years prior, certainly opponents, interest groups, or other intermediaries will remind them (Mayhew, 2004[1974]).

While signaling increased commitment to an issue should be costly for a politician who reneges on the promise, it should also be rewarding for a candidate who follows through. And, candidates who commit more strongly by making a promise on an issue should be viewed more positively than candidates who took a weaker stance on the issue before being elected. Mayhew (2004[1974]) argues that candidates leverage these fulfilled promises as credit-claiming devices that attract support from constituents. Grimmer (2013) and Grimmer, Westwood, and Messing (2014) have more clearly outlined this pathway, and demonstrated that direct attention to secured finances for the district benefits candidates. But candidates benefit not simply from presenting themselves as providing goods (in the form of monies or policies) to their districts; claiming credit for providing these goods benefits candidate valence or character assessments as well (Fiorina, 1974; Cain, Ferejohn, and Fiorina, 1987; Stein and Bickers, 1994).

Fulfilled promises should increase voter beliefs that officials will continue to fulfill promises upon reelection, as well as making valence judgments of candidates (i.e. perceptions of honesty) more positive. Conversely, fulfilled promises should decrease voter beliefs that officials will fulfill future promises and decrease perceptions of honesty about the candidate. In contrast, open-mindedness might work such that candidates who break a promise are conceived as the most open-minded, while candidates who keep their promises might be conceived as the least open-minded. Finally, during reelection campaigns, voters may make retrospective judgments about candidates simultaneously with judgments of character and future actions. Past actions constitute a signal voters may use to evaluate the candidate in comparison to other candidates as well as form judgments on future action and honesty.

Candidates who do not keep their word typically do not because of structural blockage or a natural disaster (Fishel, 1985). For US presidents, Krukones (1984) demonstrates that the bulk of the time that a president failed to follow through on campaign promises, opposition in Congress or unexpected events, such as natural disasters or conflicts, prevented him from doing so. This raises the question as to how and if politicians are able to recover from broken promises. Excuses have been studied through the lens of candidate repositioning, and strategic efforts to change position to induce greater partisan support (Karol, 2009). Although parties can strategically implement new positions, it seems quite difficult for candidates to recover from broken promises and even excuse repositioning (Tomz and Van Houweling, 2012a,b).

The distinction between promises and non-promises should translate to retrospective candidate judgments similar to the hypothesized distinctions in prospective judgments: They should polarize voter assessments of candidates. And assessments of future follow-through and character traits should match. Fulfillment will lead to more positive perspectives if the candidate promised while campaigning than if the candidate did not. Signals that candidates send during campaigns only effectively change voter opinions if voters have a mechanism through which to assess elected officials in office, and here that means judging the commitment found in statements retrospectively as well as prospectively.

2.5 CONCLUSION

Except for evidence that voters are distrustful of promises, there is little work that investigates how promises matter to voters prospectively. How the conceptual distinction in promises and non-promise matters in voter perception of candidates is thus unexplored. If voters notice these differences in statements, promises change perceptions of the level of commitment candidates portend through their position statements. And, by changing perceptions of commitment, candidates change voter opinions of candidates before candidates are elected and voters even consider how promises are fulfilled.

The theory I proposed yielded several hypotheses in this chapter concerning promises. For ease of reference, these are all summarized in Table 2.1, along with the chapter in which each hypothesis is tested. Essentially, I argued in this chapter that promises are a way for candidates to signal commitment to voters because they indicate a higher chance of potential action on an issue. This solves a problem for voters and candidates, by helping to raise the importance of issues to voters and assuring voters of candidate veracity. Voters aligning with candidates are more attracted to promises, but voters disagreeing with candidate positions are repelled by promises, leaving room for candidates to strategically implement their promises. By increasing the appearance of commitment to an issue before the election, candidates also increase costs of not following through on that issue after election, helping to ensure a signal candidates send to voters. I test this theory by first demonstrating that not only do promises exist in campaign speech (Chapter 3), voters recognize promises and assign candidates who issue them higher levels of commitment and attentiveness to the issues (Chapter 4). I then demonstrate that promises affect voter behavior by polarizing opinions of candidates both prospectively (Chapters 5 and 6) and retrospectively (Chapter 7).

TABLE 2.1 *Summary of hypotheses*

Where Measured	Concepts Tested	Hypothesis
Generally, candidates and voters differentiate between promised and non-promised position statements.		
Chapter 3	Candidate Differentiation	Candidate speech will include promise and non-promise position statements.
Chapter 4	Voters' Recognition	Voters recognize promises as distinct statements from non-promises.
	Elevated Commitment	Voters associate promises with greater levels of candidate commitment and effectiveness than non-promises.
Prospectively, promises polarize voter opinions of candidates.		
Chapter 5	Short-term preferences	Voters who agree with a candidate prefer a candidate who promises on that issue. And voters who disagree with a candidate prefer a candidate who does not promise on that issue.
	Follow-Through	Voters expect candidates who promise to be more likely to follow through than candidates who do not promise, regardless of candidate or voter position.
	Honesty	Promising increases voter expectations of honesty.
	Open-mindedness	Voters view promisers as less open-minded.
Chapter 6	Partisan leanings	Voters will rate in-party candidate promises higher than out-party candidate promises.
	Issue-party alignment	Promises along party lines will be preferred over promises against party lines, with potential for the reverse to be true.

TABLE 2.1 Summary of hypotheses, continued

Where Measured	Concepts Tested	Hypothesis
	Oversaturation	Voters who agree with a candidate prefer the candidate promise on that issue. And voters who disagree with a candidate prefer the candidate not promise on that issue.
Retrospectively, promises polarize evaluations of elected officials.		
Chapter 7	Long-term preferences	Voters prefer officials who promise to those who do not promise when the officials act in accordance with originally promised positions and voters prefer candidates who do not promise on an issue to those who promise when candidates do not act in accordance with their positions.
	Follow-through & Honesty	Generally, officials who follow through will be seen as more likely to follow through in the future and more honest than candidates who do not. Officials who promise and follow through will be seen as more likely to follow through in the future and more honest than candidates who do not promise. Officials who promise and do not follow through will be seen as less likely to follow through in the future and less honest than candidates who do not promise
	Open-mindedness	Promisers who follow through will be viewed as less open-minded than non-promisers. Promisers who do not follow through will be viewed as more open-minded than non-promisers.
	Preferences rigidity	Excuses of promise-breakers will not cause ratings of future follow-through, honesty, or open-mindedness to be as high as the ratings for a candidate who repositions but does not promise.

PART II

PROMISES AS A SPECIAL TYPE
OF POSITION-TAKING

3

Campaign Promises from 1960 to 2012

There are two streams of literature that help us understand how campaign promises affect politics. One stream has sought to understand how candidate stances on issue-positions predict electoral success, where promises are not differentiated from non-promised positions. The other addresses whether and how officials fulfill promises they made as candidates. Most of these studies have focused on party manifestos in Europe. While US parties release party platforms, and the public definitely assesses candidate linkages to parties, public evaluation in the United States remains candidate-centered (Aldrich, 1995; Fenno, 2004[1973]). Parties are a useful vehicle for candidates to organize around and utilize for their own political goals, but in the United States and elsewhere the motivations of candidates are assessed within bounds of their party affiliations, but distinctly from their parties (Aldrich, 1995).

The literature also does not provide a basic framework for how promises specifically matter to voters. Therefore this chapter seeks to ascertain how promises function as position-taking devices within actualized political speech by examining US presidential debates, giving context and external validity to the experimental chapters that follow. In so doing it builds on both the promise-fulfillment and positioning literatures by increasing the focus from statements that contain promissory language to include distinctions within candidate positions and to draw attention to promise-making in the United States.

Research documenting promise fulfillment provides evidence that issue statements vary by implied levels of commitment (e.g., Thomson et al., 2017). Since the point of understanding promise fulfillment is to demonstrate the retrospective fulfillment of promises, these studies generally focus on *whether* the statements can be assessed as fulfilled. But other studies have collected data on whether the promises feature promissory language or connection to outcomes instead of simply expressing agreement (Royed, 1996; Thomson, 2001).[1] I provide an additional lens into how positions vary between promises and non-promises, demonstrating differences in implied levels of commitment.

Further, mapping out the number of positions taken and promises made is a novel contribution in the US context. Promise-making studies that focus on US politicians either predate the most current definitions of promises, for example Fishel (1985) and Krukones (1984), or look at party platforms rather than specific candidate promises (e.g., Royed, 1996). This study investigates a wider range of statements in the United States and looks specifically at candidate speech rather than party statements. Because the US centers candidates within party politics (Aldrich, 1995), this is particularly important for examining promises in the US context. A candidate-centered documentation of campaign promises helps advance how candidates are making promises and is an important extension of the pledges literature that centers on party platforms.

While this book largely concentrates on the effects of promises on voter behavior, it is important to first ascertain whether candidates themselves make a distinction between promise and non-promise position statements. To examine this study, I present a descriptive study of candidates' statements in US presidential general election debates from 1960 to 2012. This choice of corpus offers several advantages: The debates provide a large amount of data about the range of issues discussed over several decades. They also provide equal coverage of the two dominant parties and a view of promises over a long period of time. The data demonstrates the importance of the conceptual distinction motivating my theory: Promises exist and are distinguishable as forms of position-taking.[2]

The sections below will lay out the evidence. First, I will detail the data source and selection. Second, I describe the coding procedures for the debates, which identify a promise based on the definition provided in

---

[1] These distinctions almost always delineate promissory differences on whether or not they can be judged as fulfilled – a metric that may still matter to voters hearing promises, but one which may matter less prospectively. The other delineation is between "hard" and "soft" promises, which is fundamentally a difference in promissory language.

[2] This study makes no attempt to address causal relationships between candidate promises and vote choice; it is ill-equipped to do so. In subsequent chapters, I discuss my strategy for testing a causal relationship between types of position statements and vote choice.

chapter 2. Finally, I examine the results of the coded debates, concluding that candidates take several positions throughout the debates, and a significant portion of those positions are promises.

3.1 MEASURING CANDIDATE POSITIONS: BUILDING A CORPUS

Candidates at all levels of office take positions as they campaign. But collecting, aggregating, and dissecting a broad set of campaign speeches across all ranges of offices is difficult due to both availability and selection problems. Though the theory described in Chapter 2 should translate to any level or type of office, I build a corpus of speeches composed of US presidential general election debates here because they pose several strategic advantages.

3.1.1 Presidential Election Debates as a Source

Debates provide a useful and strategic source. First, debates are widely available: There is a sufficiently large sample available for analysis, both by year and over time. The corpus begins with the earliest televised general election debates, which took place in 1960. Most election years, there are three presidential general election debates, although incumbent presidents did not participate in debates until 1980, and thus the corpus is empty for 1964, 1968, and 1972.[3] The first incumbent president to participate in a debate is Gerald Ford in 1980, which means that there are no presidential debates for 1964, 1968, or 1972. This results in a total of thirty general election debates that I am able to use for this analysis, all of which lasted 60–90 minutes.[4] One or more prominent media figures serve as moderators. The format of each debate varies slightly, but most allowed for an opening and/or closing statement from each of the candidates, questions posed to the candidates, and a short time

---

[3] I am excluding the nine vice presidential debates that occurred between 1960 and 2012. While it is conceivable that voters would connect promises made by vice presidential candidates to the presidential candidates, there are differences in language and frequency between the presidential and vice presidential candidates. Excluding them helps to maintain the consistency of the sample.

[4] Four of the debates include an independent candidate: a debate between Ronald Reagan and John Anderson in 1980, and three debates among George H. W. Bush, Bill Clinton, and Ross Perot in 1992. Since, in later analysis, I show that party does not seem to have an effect in the level of promise-making and because the inclusion of an independent candidate does not change the structure of the debate, I include both Anderson and Perot cases in the full tallies but exclude them from the candidate-specific analyses.

for rebuttal of opponents' responses. (The Appendix provides a more detailed description of each debate.)

Second, the purpose of debates lends an important reason for the primary focus on them: Namely, the educational impact of debates is large. Debates are to educate voters of the campaign's agendas, and they are successful in reducing uncertainty in voters who do not know the candidates' issue positions regardless of education, political interest, or a number of other demographic variables (Lemert, 1993). (Jamieson and Birdsell (1988) give a good review on the effect of debates.) Ultimately, candidates debate to " 'without reserve, ...dispel the clouds of falsehood' " (Walters, 1976). Debates, then, encourage the candidates to clarify their positions to the public.

A third advantage of debates is that they are highly visible, which means that the candidates believe the electorate will observe their statements and may act on them. Presidential general election debates are widely televised on major broadcasting stations and attract a large at-home audience (Carlin, 2009). Viewership averages 58.8 million viewers for the debates in the corpus, reflecting steady growth from 1960 to 1988. While the number who watch general election debates live has never returned to its height in 1988 (Kraus, 2013), modern-day voters may view them later, read transcripts, or view parts of them, and it seems likely that candidates view them as important. In later years, they are transcribed immediately and replayed on various sources throughout the Internet. By contrast, stump speeches and advertisements, are only seen in select areas of the country, where the candidate decides to present them, and viewed by a limited audience, even if they are reported on nationally. They are also much shorter and tend to be targeted toward a specific audience and topic. Thus, debates are the forum through which voters are most likely to learn about political positions (Just, Crigler, and Wallach, 1990) and candidates have the opportunity to give a more complete picture of their positions in comparison to other types of campaign speech. Candidates are likely to expect voters to pay attention to any positions they take in debates.

Finally, debates generally touch on many of the issues discussed over the entire course of a campaign. While debates are usually focused on a topic domain such as foreign or domestic affairs, there are still several topics within those categories that candidates are asked to address. In addition, since an external moderator chooses the questions, candidates will have an opportunity to interact with a range of issues, as they might in town halls, interviews with media, or direct response to voters.

Importantly, while these last two points highlight why debates may be useful, it is important to note that debates come with limitations. Certainly, candidates may issue promises to different crowds – though this is certainly much less likely in more recent elections. For example, Mitt Romney's comments on income tax and the "47 percent" were intended for a private group of donors but were heard by the nation at large (Mullis, 2012).

Of course, debates do not capture every single position statement that candidates make over the course of a campaign, but they offer a broad representation of what issues a candidate decides to make promises about. In short, debates act as a summary of a campaign:

Debates are essentially the focal point of the campaign. A campaign is, in and of itself, an extended debate with a variety of candidate messages that state positions on issues, recall past accomplishments, emphasize credentials, make comparisons to the opponent(s), criticize opponent's positions or records. Debates often include references to what was said in other campaign messages, and candidates extend and further refine their messages form the campaign trail during a debate. (Carlin, 2009, p. 9)

They also provide a useful snapshot of campaigns (Erikson and Wlezien, 2012), and even though candidates do not choose all the questions, they are able to emphasize their agenda and ignore discussing positions (Carlin, 2009).[5] In sum, debates are a unique campaign event, but one which gives a compelling overview of what candidates say and what they do not say. I have similar expectations that what I find here will apply to other forms of candidate speech and that debates should provide an accurate representation of a broader type of speeches. As such, they are a perfect opportunity to examine the existence and availability of promised and non-promised positions.

---

[5] This also points to another differentiated feature of using debates: While debates cover many categories broadly, it would be difficult to cover any topic in-depth. Candidates may not fully explain the minutia of their positions but still tend to give broad overviews of their positions and often refer to other speeches, written plans, or websites that more clearly delineate the particulars of their plans. The availability of data allows for more comprehensive coverage than might otherwise be attained and outweighs these concerns, which would be more important for an investigation into how specific and detailed candidates were on various issues.

3.1.2 Identifying Candidate Positions in Debates

My corpus is comprised of debate transcripts from the American Presidency Project, the Commission on Presidential Debates, and the *New York Times* Archives.[6] I aggregated, reformatted, and then read the transcripts under the series of rules described here. This involved, first, locating candidate appeals – situations when candidates make specific references to their positions on policy – then classifying the appeal as a promise or a non-promise position statement. This section describes the criteria to determine whether a statement was a position statement, and the next describes the criteria to determine whether the statement was a promise.

3.1.3 Coding Promise and Non-promise Statements

To distinguish campaign appeals, I coded the debates following a content analysis method described by Geer (2006) and Sulkin (2011). The unit of analysis is the specific appeal the candidate is making, rather than a whole debate or even each answer that a candidate makes. (The minimum length of appeal that I use is the sentence.) This is important because while a candidate may be asked a question about taxes, the answer may include positions on education or social security as well as taxes. Like Sulkin (2011) (and unlike Geer (2006)), I consider an appeal described over several sentences to be the description of one position taken.[7] But if a candidate returned to a topic after discussing a second topic, I considered it a separate appeal. After identifying appeals, I determined if each was a promise or a non-promise position statement.

I now turn to how promise and non-promise position statements were determined based on my coding rules. To do so, understanding the operational definition of promise versus non-promise is essential. Promises are statements the candidate makes about what he will do (or not do) on a

---

[6] There were a few errors in each of the 1988 debates (places with obvious insertions or deletions of statements). Where these occurred, I reconciled the transcripts with the *New York Times* Archive Debate Transcripts and communicated with the American Presidency Project to correct the errors.

[7] For instance, two statements described in the following section are useful examples. The entire statement Gerald Ford made explaining why he vetoed a bill that would limit strip mining and giving two reasons for his veto represent a single position. Mitt Romney's statement that Syria is important consists of multiple sentences, yet reflects the same topic.

particular issue if elected to office or what will occur if he is elected.[8] These are firm statements about the candidate's specific plans of action. They may use promissory language, such as "I promise," "I pledge," or "I guarantee." However, statements did not have to include promissory language as long as they indicated what the candidates would do if elected or indicated an outcome that would happen.[9] Projections to actions or occurrences in the future either specifically referencing being elected or for actions contingent on the candidate's getting elected were classified as promise statements. In contrast, non-promise statements included position statements captured in this analysis that are not promises. These were statements candidates made to voters excluding any expectation of action.

3.2 CODING RELIABILITY

Great care was taken to apply consistent coding methods across all debates. Instead of using multiple coders, I coded the debates twice.[10] I also examined my agreement with two sets of two coders who read ten debates each using the more general coding rubric.[11]

To ensure coding reliability, I use a text analytic method to examine that the content of the promise and non-promise position statements varies as their definitions would predict. For instance, promises should use active voice and express a candidate's anticipated actions, whereas non-promise positions should use less active voice.

---

[8] I use the binary coding scheme of promise and non-promise. While it is probable that there are more types of position statements, this study's objective is not to observe the distinctions among them all. My goal is to first demonstrate that there are multiple ways to take a position, including with a promise and without a promise. A future study can further investigate the subtleties between different position-taking methods.

[9] In this study, I ignore quality and credibility of promise statements, and consider only a single level of whether or not a candidate is making a promise.

[10] The first time I coded the debates in reverse chronological order, and the second time I coded the debates in chronological order. The general findings described below remain the same, which indicates that the results are not due simply to learning the coding rules over time.

[11] For the alternative coding, I used a more general unit of analysis: a candidate's answer to a moderator's question. The alternative coders recorded each time in the ten debates when the candidate made a promise in their estimation. (This meant disagreement about which word starts or ends the promise would not be recorded, but only about whether a promise exists at all.) The coder agreement rate is 87 percent with each other, and 92 percent with me, in both greater than chance would predict. (See Lombard, Snyder-Duch, and Bracken (2002).)

3.2.1 Dictionary Method

A dictionary method compares words in a corpus to word categories from a dictionary, and determines the proportion of words from the corpus that fall in a specific category. Grimmer and Stewart (2013) give an overview of the method.[12] For each word in the category, m, ($m = 1, \ldots, M$), there is an associated score, s_m. If the statement contains the word category, $s_m = 1$, and $s_m = -1$ if it does not. If the number of words in the document i is $N_i = \sum_M^{m=1} W_{im}$, then,

$$t_i = \sum_{m=1}^{M} \frac{s_m W_{im}}{N_i}.$$

I used the *Harvard Inquirer*,[13] a well-known dictionary that contains many categories of words. I then compared the words contained in each type of position statement with the words found in the dictionary. The *Harvard Inquirer* contains more word categories than would be prudent to use in this study. As such, I selected the word categories in which we should expect to see salient differences between promise and non-promise position statements. I examined action-orientation, motivation, and knowledge categories. In particular, I expect there to be a greater representation of active and motivation-related words in the promise category, because the commitment to a future action should be active. For example, words included in these categories are "Act" or "Undertake."

In addition, "Need" and "Try" both describe activities that express intentions and activities needed to be taken to achieve a goal. In contrast, I expect a greater representation of descriptive knowledge among non-

---

[12] One general criticism of dictionary methods is that they do not perform well when the dictionary is not specific to the subject matter. In this case, because the candidates are covering a variety of issues, they discuss many different subjects for a general audience. Even though the speech is within a political context, a general dictionary is sufficient to capture the overarching rhetoric. Moreover, the goal with this analysis is not to document the content of the positions but to say how they differ from each other. It is possible that the categories where promises are made are substantively different, but the goal of this analysis is simply to identify what types of language differentiates non-promise positions from promises, independent of the topic. As such, a general dictionary was more useful than a political dictionary or a dictionary specific to the general topic of each debate would be.

[13] See www.wjh.harvard.edu/inquirer/.

TABLE 3.1 *Dictionary word categories and predictions by statement*

Topic	Dictionary	Definition	Statement
Active	Active	Implies active orientation	Promise
Motivation	Need	Expression of intent	Promise
	Try	Activities taken to reach goal	Promise
	Means	Methods used in achieving goals	Promise
	Goal	End-states	Promise
	Persist	Indicates endurance	Promise
Cognitive	Causal	Dependence of one item on another	Position
Orientation	Think	Thought process	Position
	Know	Awareness or unawareness	Position
	Ought	Words indicating moral imperative	Position

Source: The Harvard Inquirer.

promise statements, because that indicates the candidate understands the topic and what the candidate thinks about it rather than what the candidate would do about it. For example, some of the words included in these categories are "Support" or "Favor." Knowledge category words indicate that the candidate understands and asserts what they think on a topic, consistent with the definition that non-promise statements describe only how the candidate describes a position a topic. Each of the categories contains subcategories; these are presented along with a definition and the statement that I would predict to be most closely associated with that topic in Table 3.1.

To compare each of the categories, I regressed the dictionary category against the proportion of each category found in the position statements,

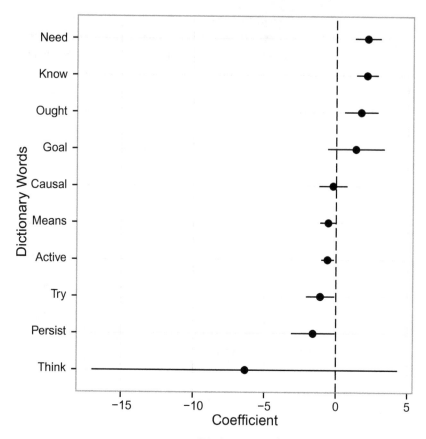

FIGURE 3.1 Dictionary results

These results show the coefficient and 95% confidence interval of the difference between the $t_{promises}$ and $t_{non-promises}$. Negative values indicate a greater correlation among promises, positive values indicate a greater correlation found among non-promises.

t_i in the equation, by one category against the other categories. Figure 3.1 shows the results.

I also compared the difference between promises and non-promise positions alone, since the differences between these two categories are the most salient. In particular, the cognitive orientation words are more likely to be found in non-promise position statements: "Know" and "Ought." As predicted, these words reflect a slightly larger discussion of knowledge about an issue than a promise statement might. Active and motivation words tend to be reflected most by promises, including the categories "Try," "Active," "Persist," and "Means."

The two exceptions to the predicted category associations are "Need" and "Goal," both of which represent motivation words and were predicted to be more represented in promises. A closer look at each of these categories indicates that they need not necessarily represent action. Since "Goal" simply describes the end-state, and not the means, effort, or sincerity that the candidate will use to get to the goal, the candidate could do so by conveying means of action. Similarly, "Need" expresses urgency to do something, but does not necessarily indicate an action will be taken, only that it might be desirable. Thus, the original mis-categorization of these words need not go against my theory, and does contribute to a better understanding of how positions differ.

In sum, the analysis both confirms the accuracy of my coding predictions and highlights the differences between non-promise position statements and promises. That is, the dictionary categories most often represented in promise statements are action- and motivation-oriented, while the categories represented in the non-promise statements tend to only indicate the description of an issue. In general, this underlines the use of commitment language in the description of a promise. Moreover, it confirms that the defined coding distinctions are in fact present in the coded documents.

3.3 RESULTS: PROMISES IN THE DEBATES

I report the coding results by first examining the frequency of each type of position statement taken in each year. Because the number[14] and length[15] of debates vary by election year, I standardize the rates of statements by looking at the proportion of statements made in an election year rather than looking at the absolute number of each position type. (A description of the debates, their location, and participants can be found in the Appendix.) I also group the debates together by year to help control for

---

[14] There are four general election debates with the major parties represented in 1960. In 1980 and 1984, there are two debates with the major parties represented. In 1988, there are only two debates. All other years had three debates between the majority-party, presidential candidates.

[15] In 1960, the debates were 60 minutes long. Most other years the debates were 90 minutes long.

the types of topics covered. Many debates were focused on domestic or foreign policy issues, and grouping the debates together by year allows me to normalize for the range of topics covered by a particular candidate. Finally, to control for debate length, and to calculate the proportion of the debate for that statement, I divide the number of words within a statement by the number of words in the debate year. In addition, different moderators and different debate formats could potentially affect results.[16] I have done this analysis by excluding and including moderators with no overall differences in the results. The results reported here exclude moderator statements in the calculations of debate year length.

3.3.1 The Frequency of Promise-Making and Position-Taking in Debates

Throughout the debates, candidates made both promise and non-promise statements. And promise statements sometimes occurred with promissory language. For instance, although his "read my lips" statement was far more famous, George H. W. Bush also stated, "the answer is to discipline both the executive branch and the congressional branch by holding the line on taxes. So I'm pledged to do that" (Bush, 1988). More frequently, promises occurred without promissory language, as did John Kerry's promise: "I'm going to give you [voters] a tax cut" (Kerry, 2004). The non-promise statements did occur as well, including what candidates felt about positions without indicating how they would act. For instance, Gerald Ford took this position: "I would prefer in that tax bill to have an additional tax cut and a further limitation on federal spending" (Ford, 1976a). Although it is clear that Ford thought there should be changes to the tax bill, he did not emphasize his own commitment to realize the additional components of the tax bill.

Importantly, as anticipated, candidates also avoided discussing positions by simply talking about the subject more generally as Mitt Romney did when asked to talk about American involvement in Syria: "Well, let's

---

[16] Some debates had a single moderator that asked the candidates all of the questions. Others, particularly the earlier debates, had a main moderator who directed other media figures to ask questions of the candidates. In still other debates, there was a town hall format with viewers who asked the questions. Each of these formats leaves candidates with different amount of times to speak and make position statements.

step back and talk about what's happening in Syria and how important it is," he began (Romney, 2012). Or, a candidate, instead of answering with his position, might talk about their own record or criticize their opponent's record. For example, when Gerald Ford was asked to explain his position on environmental issues, he did not tell voters anything about his position except the importance of the environment with respect to jobs, saying he had vetoed a particular bill because it would have cost more than a hundred thousand jobs in coal.

First, let me set the record straight. I vetoed the strip mining bill, Mr. Kraft, because it was the overwhelming consensus of knowledgeable people that that strip mining bill would have meant the loss of literally thousands of jobs, something around 140,000 jobs. Number two, that strip mining bill would have severely set back our need for more coal, and Governor Carter has said repeatedly that coal is the resource that we need to use more in the effort to become independent of the Arab oil supplies. (Ford, 1976*b*)

Candidates also essentially ignore questions, as John McCain did when a moderator asked him what programs he would be willing to cut to help balance the budget. His response began, "I just want to get back to this home ownership," deflecting a question about the national budget to reference household budgets (McCain, 2008). The fact that debates allow candidates to selectively make, or ignore, appeals even to the point of ignoring a moderator's question corroborates the point that studying candidate speech patterns in debates does not overexaggerate the types of positions that candidates are willing to take in their campaigns.

Figure 3.2 shows candidate statements by type over each year in my corpus. In most years, candidates identified positions, without promises, more frequently than with promises. The proportion of statements that present a non-promised position increased from 1960 to 2012. Moreover, the proportion of promise statements has drastically increased over the same time period. In 1960, candidates spent about an eighth of the debate clarifying their position on a certain issue.[17] Two percent of the debate time was spent making promises, a rate of about four promises per debate, or sixteen promises by both candidates over the

---

[17] A large portion of the remaining time was spent on qualifying candidate character or examining records.

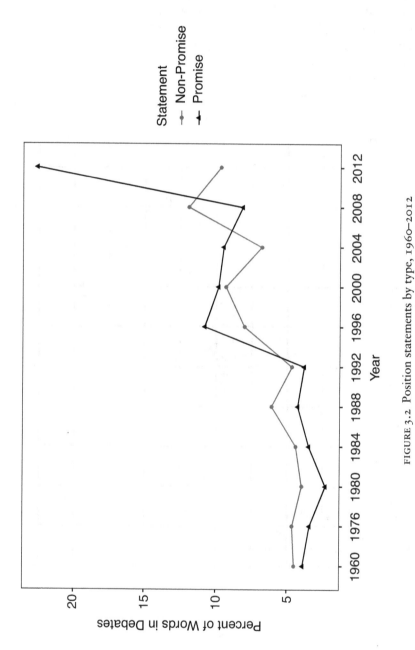

FIGURE 3.2 Position statements by type, 1960–2012

This figure shows the proportion of each type of statement. The numbers are averaged across year and normalized by the average number of words in each debate year in order to control for variations in topic content, number of debates per year, and length of debate.

election period. In contrast, in the 2012 debates, about half of the debate was spent clarifying non-promise positions, with about 24 percent of the statements being promises. This translates to about 36 promises made on average during each debate, or 144 made in the three debates between Barack Obama and Mitt Romney.

These figures do not remove time the candidates spend greeting the crowd (or questioners), discussions of candidates' own records, criticisms of their opponent, and each candidates' characters. They also include time spent discussing the issues very broadly without taking a position on the issue. In context, then, one-fifth of a debate devoted to discussing promises and one-half of a debate spent discussing issue positions are considerable time periods.[18]

This data reveals that the way that candidates take positions has changed over time in the debates. The rate at which promise and non-promise positions are made increases substantially only after 1992; prior to 1992, there is very little change in differences between promise and non-promise position statements.[19] Past work documenting position statements indicated that candidates rarely take positions (Page, 1978; McGinnis, 1969). Although it is hard to determine frequency, what I find is that position-taking is a notable portion of time in debates. Documenting that both promise and non-promise policy statements exist in debates is an important step in confirming the importance of my theory, however, as this finding documents that candidates do vary policy statements in candidate speeches. Moreover, what I find here, the growth of both types of speech, means that the distinction between promises and non-promises is nontrivial for understanding current position-taking strategies.

---

[18] It is a bit difficult to disaggregate all of the things candidates spend time talking about during a debate. I have coded time spent discussing the other candidates' positions and records as well as time spent discussing their own records. Nonetheless, it is possible for these categories to overlap, which would make it difficult to understand the time spent on each activity as a part of a whole.

[19] This finding might seem inconsistent with the findings of Fishel (1985), who discusses promises in candidate acceptance speeches. While he finds that candidate positions increased steadily from 1920 to 1980, I find that they remain largely the same through the time for which our study periods overlap. First, it is possible that the increase in positions from 1920 to 1980 is driven by a larger increase in the mid-point of his data collection. Additionally, acceptance speeches lengthened over his period of focus as debates do in mine, yet there is no correction for changes in timing as I have tried to do. In addition, he aggregates both promises and non-promised positions, so his results may be true but minimized by our different focuses.

3.3.2 Candidates and Promising

Now, I look at candidate-specific information with respect to promising. Which candidates have made the most promises over time? This data is displayed in Figure 3.3. The bar plot shows the proportion of time each candidate spends making promises and taking non-promise positions. The candidates are ordered from the most time spent on promises to the least. Mitt Romney spent the greatest proportion of the debates making promises and Ronald Reagan spent the least.

As a general rule, incumbents took positions with fewer promises than challengers ($\mu_{incumbent} = 1.9$, $\mu_{nonincumbent} = 3.0$, $p = 0.06$), although Jimmy Carter took more than his own challenger, Ronald Reagan. At the same time, incumbents made more promises in their reelection debates than in their own first debates, except George H. W. Bush. Perhaps this was because his breaking of his "read my lips: no new taxes" promise had produced so much criticism.

While most incumbent candidates made more promises in their second election cycle than their first (all but George H. W. Bush and Jimmy Carter), they still made fewer promises than their challengers (except for Jimmy Carter who made more promises than Ronald Reagan). That a non-incumbent candidate should be more likely to take a position and make a promise is not surprising and may underline the use of promises as commitment devices. Incumbent candidates have a more visible record that they can point to, or are called to defend, in the course of the campaign. If sitting presidents make fewer promises, it is possible that they need them less, because they have a record that can be used to demonstrate how they might act in the future to voters. Moreover, incumbents are less likely to identify further positions (Milita, Ryan, and Simas, 2014). That incumbents are less likely to promise has also been noted among congressional candidates (Druckman, Kifer, and Parkin, 2009). In general, then, it would make sense that incumbent candidates are more likely to address records and character, than are challengers.[20]

Next, I consider the differences in promise-making rates between winners and losers. In general, winners did promise more than losers but not significantly so ($\mu_{win} = 1.8$, $\mu_{lose} = 3.4$, $p = 0.3$). Winners, other than Ronald Reagan in 1980, promised more frequently than losers before 1992. After 1992, winners other than George W. Bush in 2000, promised less frequently (and whether he won that election has been debated). This 1992 cutoff coincides with the rapid increase of promises.

---

[20] However, all challengers have a previous public record of some kind, albeit in a different office. The defense of the public record requires different attention for challengers.

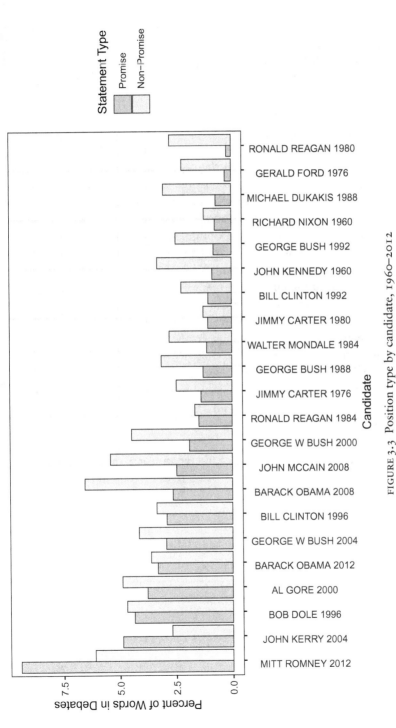

FIGURE 3.3 Position type by candidate, 1960–2012

This figure shows the percentage of each type of statement by candidate. The numbers are averaged across year and normalized by the average number of words in each debate year in order to control for variations in topic content, number of debates per year, and length of debate.

Although the analysis here cannot determine the cause of the shift, two possibilities are worth mentioning.

First, the sponsor of the debates changed in 1992. In 1960, the television networks (ABC, CBS, and NBC) sponsored the presidential debates. The American League of Women Voters sponsored the next set of debates, in 1976, as well as those in 1980, 1984, and 1988. In 1992, the League announced that they would no longer host the debates and the newly formed Commission on Presidential Debates took over. Debate sponsors act as mediators between the campaigns in order to set dates and rules for the campaigns.[21] It is possible that the potential switch of the moderators altered the debate environment. However, this is unlikely because, as Minow and LaMay (2008) note, the rules in the debates remained largely the same, and the Commission on Presidential Debates took actions in moderating the format and rules for the debates much like the League of Women Voters had. The commission also faced similar difficulties the league had in setting rules for the debates and continuing to attract audiences. Additionally, the campaigns continued to be the driving force behind the debate rules as they had been before (Kraus, 2013).

More likely, the shift was endemic to the candidate strategies themselves and changes that occurred in campaigning in 1992. The way that candidates discussed issues shifted over the course of the debates. Earlier in the debate corpus, candidates seemed more willing to discuss issues abstractly and generally. Later candidates addressed issues more directly (Jamieson and Birdsell, 1988). The discussion of candidate character in the debates declined in 1992 specifically: There were seventeen fewer questions about candidate character in 1992 than in 1988 and it never returned to the earlier levels. This frees up time to discuss issues (Kraus, 2013). Another 1992 event was Bill Clinton's appearance on late night television – the first for any presidential candidate. Changes in television viewing have altered presidential campaign strategy (Baum, 2005; Baum and Kernell, 1999), including the rise of "talk show" campaign strategies and the prevalence of candidate appearances on late night shows (Parkin, 2014). These factors might similarly induce

---

[21] The campaigns have set a very rigid and specific contract before they engage in televised debates, particularly as debates first started. Rules involved specifying not only question content and response duration but also camera angles, the number and types of camera shots that are permissible, and situation of the candidates. See Minow and LaMay (2008) and Kraus (2013) for a couple of good histories on the development of the debates, the rules in them, and the laws concerning them.

promise-making as an attention-seeking strategy (Kostadinova, 2013), despite potential repercussions in revealing issue positions (Milita, Ryan, and Simas, 2014). Additionally, the 1992 shift corresponds to other changes in rhetoric by presidential candidates, including an increased use of mandate claims and promise-based rhetoric post-election (Azari, 2014). The changes in promise-making may be a function of the rhetorical changes in the political climate over the last sixty years.

3.4 CONCLUSION

The goal of this chapter was to investigate the presence of promises in candidate position-taking and whether the distinction between promise and non-promise positions is a nontrivial classification. I strictly defined promises as statements expressing future policy actions or outcomes and non-promises as statements lacking actions or outcomes. In order to capture a measure of positions statements, I created a corpus of general presidential debates from 1960 through 2012. The data presented here demonstrates not only that promises exist but also that the distinction between promises and non-promises is an important conceptual contribution to understanding position-taking by candidates that is not an artifact of experiments or theory, but exists in real campaign speech.

First, the data demonstrates that promises are well represented among position statements, and in the past twenty years, they have become increasingly prominent. The proportion of promises in debates remained a relatively small portion of position-taking until 1992. Given past research that indicates policy positions are rarely discussed, it is important to recognize that position statements take up a worthwhile portion of debates. Perhaps even more important for this study is the evidence that promises comprise a noticeable proportion of candidate statements.

Second, the conceptual distinction occurs across all candidate types: winners, losers, incumbents, and challengers. However, incumbents routinely make fewer promises than challengers in the same election. This finding is particularly useful because it comports with behavior other studies have attributed to incumbents (Druckman, Kifer, and Parkin, 2009), helping to validate the results described here.

One important question about choosing debates as representation of candidate speech is whether lessons learned from the analysis here would generalize to other aspects of candidate speech and candidates running for different offices. This indeed is an important limitation: The debates here are not the only form of candidate speech used and allow focus only on the race for the presidency. If the lessons learned here were limited only to presidential candidates and debates, we learn something interesting and important about American elections, and particularly about presidential campaigning. However, I believe the general patterns emerging in this chapter are likely true of candidates for other offices throughout US government, for several reasons. First, candidates share similar motivations regardless of the office they are running for (Calvert, 1985; Wittman, 1983). Candidates want to win the offices they are running for, and often candidates want to realize a personal policy goal (Sulkin, 2011). As much as utilizing different types of position statements is a strategic endeavor by politicians, I expect that candidates would use them similarly (even if the ratio of promises to non-promises changes) regardless of the level of office. Second, an important factor that differentiates presidential candidates from other candidates is the visibility of their statements and promises. Although this might change candidates' opportunity to emphasize various aspects of their platforms by promising or offering non-promise statements, they are still likely to take those opportunities they have. As we consider the changes the Internet, 24-hour news cycles, and social media have made on the political landscape, it is not certain that debates are necessarily more visible than other types of campaign speech. Third, because the media or an opponent has potential to draw attention to any statement a candidate makes, candidates are very careful in how they present themselves even in more controlled environments (Druckman, Kifer, and Parkin, 2014). Finally, given the data presented in Chapters 5, 6, and 7, it is unlikely that candidates would over-promise in these debates. At worst, candidates would spend more time discussing policy without promising in the debates than in other forms of speech, but given media and voter interaction, debates are not the only forum in which candidates are pushed to discuss policies on which they do not want to commit (Milita, Ryan, and Simas, 2014). Thus, we can anticipate that even on low-traffic campaign websites, the images that candidates present can be expected to be as regulated as in positions where they are highly visible, such as a stump speech or a debate. As a result, I expect candidates for all levels of office to differentiate between making promises on issues and discussing positions without making promises.

This chapter, then, provided the first set of evidence that not only do promises exist as distinct forms of position-taking but they are also increasingly common. Here, I demonstrate that both types of statements are represented in candidate speech, which is important to prove that the voters might respond differently to them. In Chapter 4, I provide additional evidence that the conceptual and theoretical distinction of promises exists. I show that voters react differently to candidates whose position statements include and omit promises, and demonstrate that promises affect voter behavior.

APPENDIX

3.A Presidential Debates

Presidential debates in some variation have occurred well before the advent of television. I use the televised presidential debates because the format of the debates is similar throughout the entirety of the debates. In addition, the debates give an informative snapshot of the focal points of the different campaigns. In Table 3.2, I share the information for each of the debates.

TABLE 3.2 *Presidential debate information*

Date	Length (min)	Viewers (mil)	Sponsor	Moderator, Questioners	Candidates	Format
September 23, 1960	60	66.4	Networks (ABC, CBS, NBC)	Howard Smith, Sander Vanocur, Charles Warren, Stuart Novins	John Kennedy, Richard Nixon	Opening, Question and Answer with Optional Rebuttal, Closing
October 7, 1960	60	61.9	Networks (ABC, CBS, NBC)	Frank McGee, Paul Niven, Edward Morgan Alvin Spivak, Harold Levy	John Kennedy, Richard Nixon	Question and Answer with Optional Rebuttal
October 13, 1960	60	63.7	Networks (ABC, CBS, NBC)	Bill Shadele, Frank McGee, Charles Van Fremd, Douglass Cater, Roscoe Drummond	John Kennedy, Richard Nixon	Question and Answer with Optional Rebuttal
October 21, 1960	60	60.4	Networks (ABC, CBS, NBC)	Quincy Howe, Frank Singiser, John Edwards, Walter Cronkite	John Kennedy, Richard Nixon	Opening, Question and Answer with Optional Rebuttal, Closing
September 23, 1976	90	69.7	League of Women Voters	Edwin Newman, Frank Reynolds, James Gannon, Elizabeth Drew	Jimmy Carter, Gerald Ford	Question and Answer with Rebuttal, Closing

Date	Minutes	Rating	Sponsor	Panelists	Participants	Format
October 6, 1976	90	63.9	League of Women Voters	Pauline Frederick, Max Frankel, Henry Trewitt, Richard Valeriana	Jimmy Carter, Gerald Ford	Question and Answer with Rebuttal and Optional Follow-up, Closing
October 22, 1976	90	62.7	League of Women Voters	Barbara Walters, Joseph Kraft, Robert Maynard, Jack Nelson	Jimmy Carter, Gerald Ford	Question and Answer with Rebuttal and Optional Follow-up, Closing
September 21, 1980	60	80.6	League of Women Voters	Bill Moyers, Carol Loomis, Daniel Greenberg, Charles Cordy, Lee May, Jane Bryant Quinn, Soma Golden	Ronald Reagan, John Anderson	Question and Answer with Rebuttal, Closing
October 28, 1980	90	65.1	League of Women Voters	Howard Smith, Marvin Stone, Harry Ellis, William Hilliard, Barbara Walters	Jimmy Carter, Ronald Reagan	First Half: Question and Answer with Rebuttal and Optional Follow-up; Second Half: Question and Answer with two Rebuttals
October 7, 1984	90	67.3	League of Women Voters	Barbara Walters, James Wieghart, Diane Sawyer, Fred Barnes	Walter Mondale, Ronald Reagan	Question and Answer with Rebuttal and Follow-up, Closing

TABLE 3.2 *Continued*

Date	Length (min)	Viewers (mil)	Sponsor	Moderator, Questioners	Candidates	Format
October 21, 1984	90	65.1	League of Women Voters	Edwin Newman, Georgie Anne Geyer, Marvin Kalb, Mortan Kondracke	Walter Mondale, Ronald Reagan	Question and Answer with Rebuttal and Follow-up, Closing
September 25, 1988	90	67.3	CPD	Jim Lehrer, John Mashek, Peter Jennings, Ann Groer	Michael Dukakis, George H. W. Bush	Question and Answer with Rebuttal and Follow-up, Closing
October 13, 1988	90	62.4	CPD	Bernard Shaw, Andrea Mitchell, Ann Compton, Margaret Warner	Michael Dukakis, George H. W. Bush	Question and Answer with Rebuttal and Follow-up, Closing
October 11, 1992	90	69.9	CPD	Jim Lehrer, Sander Vanocur, Ann Compton, John Mashek	Bill Clinton, George H. W. Bush, Ross Perot	Question and Answer with Rebuttal, Closing
October 15, 1992	90	66.9	CPD	Carole Simpson, Voters	Bill Clinton, George H. W. Bush, Ross Perot	Town Hall Questions and Closing Statements

Date	Length	Sponsor	Rating	Candidates	Moderator(s)	Format
October 19, 1992	90	CPD	46.1	Bill Clinton, George H. W. Bush, Ross Perot	Jim Lehrer, Gene Gibbons, Helen Thomas, Susan Rook	First Half: Single Moderator Question and Answer with Rebuttal; Second Half: Panelists Question and Answer, Closing
October 6, 1996	90	CPD	36.3	Bill Clinton, Bob Dole	Jim Lehrer	Opening, Question and Answer with Rebuttal, Closing
October 16, 1996	90	CPD	46.6	Bill Clinton, Bob Dole	Jim Lehrer, Voters	Opening, Town Hall Questions and Answer with Rebuttal, Closing
October 3, 2000	90	CPD	37.5	Al Gore, George W. Bush	Jim Lehrer	Question and Answer with Rebuttal, Closing
October 11, 2000	90	CPD	37.7	Al Gore, George W. Bush	Jim Lehrer	Question and Answer with Rebuttal, Closing
October 17, 2000	90	CPD	62.4	Al Gore, George W. Bush	Jim Lehrer	Town Hall Questions and Answer with Rebuttal, Closing
September 30, 2004	90	CPD	46.7	John Kerry, George W. Bush	Jim Lehrer	Question and Answer with Rebuttal and Discussion Extensions

TABLE 3.2 *Continued*

Date	Length (min)	Viewers (mil)	Sponsor	Moderator, Questioners	Candidates	Format
October 8, 2004	90	51.1	CPD	Charles Gibson, Voters	John Kerry, George W. Bush	Town Hall Questions and Answer with Rebuttal and Extensions, Closing
October 13, 2004	90	52.4	CPD	Bob Schieffer	John Kerry, George W. Bush	Question and Answer with Rebuttal and Discussion Extensions
September 26, 2008	90	63.2	CPD	Jim Lehrer	Barack Obama, John McCain	Question and Answer with Open Discussions
October 7, 2008	90	56.5	CPD	Tom Brokaw, Voters	Barack Obama, John McCain	Question and Answer with Open Discussions
October 15, 2008	90	58.8	CPD	Bob Schieffer	Barack Obama, John McCain	Question and Answer with Open Discussions
October 3, 2012	90	67.2	CPD	Jim Lehrer	Barack Obama, Mitt Romney	Question and Answer with Open Discussions
October 16, 2012	90	65.6	CPD	Candy Crowley, Voters	Barack Obama, Mitt Romney	Question and Answer with Rebuttal and Discussion Extensions
October 22, 2012	90	59.2	CPD	Bob Schieffer	Barack Obama, Mitt Romney	Question and Answer with Open Discussions

4

Voter Perceptions of Promises

One of the major contributions of this book is to show that language alone can create the appearance of variations in commitment, and that voters understand position statements differently if they are made with a promise. The conceptual distinction requires that candidate speech distinguishes promises from non-promises and that voters recognize this distinction. While Chapter 3 documented that candidates distinguish promises as a specific type of position statement in campaign speech, this chapter demonstrates that voters also perceive differences between promises and non-promises. In so doing, it uses the definition of promises provided in Chapter 2. As such, this chapter also serves as a check that the experimental manipulations on promises in subsequent chapters induce changes in candidate evaluations because voters perceive differences in commitment between promises and non-promise issue statements.

I present the results from two surveys that examine voters' responses to promises by asking how they understand various statements made by candidates for public office. Both, like the rest of the book, center on promises made about gun control. Therefore, the next section explains why I use survey experiments to understand the effects of promise-making and why I focus on gun control as an issue through which to explore campaign promises. Descriptions of the two definitional tasks that I use to measure voter opinions about promise statements and non-promise statements follow. Study 1 tests if voter conceptions of promises match the definition of promises in this book. (See Table 4.1.) Study 2 tests if voters attach a greater level of commitment to promises, as argued in Chapter 2.

TABLE 4.1 *List of hypotheses and experiments*

Hypothesis	Study Testing Hypothesis
Voter recognition of promises	
(1) Voters recognize position statements with attached actions as promises.	Study 1: Definitions
(2) Promissory language is not required for an issue position to be considered a promise.	Study 1: Definitions
Promises elevate commitment	
(3) Voters assign greater levels of commitment and effectiveness to promise statements than non-promise statements.	Study 2: Commitment
(4) Promissory language does not affect perceptions of commitment associated with a promise.	Study 2: Commitment

Note: This table enumerates and summarizes a list of hypotheses fully argued in Chapter 2, and depicts which study tests which of the hypotheses.

This chapter provides evidence that voters can identify the distinction between promise and non-promise statements. Specifically, voters define promises as I do and distinguish position statements by whether they constitute promises. Further, I demonstrate that the distinction between promise and non-promise statements is not simply a matter of differences in words but important in recognizing how voters understand candidate commitment and effectiveness.

4.1 RATIONALE FOR THE MEASURING THE EFFECT OF PROMISES

Observational studies have been critical in understanding the fulfillment of promises, and have demonstrated evidence that promissory representation exists,[1] but such studies would not illuminate the prospective effect of promises themselves. Elections are quite noisy, and it would be difficult, if not impossible, to cleanly measure promises among the many intermediaries that may affect voter behavior. Instead, I turn to survey experiments, which elsewhere have been instrumental in studies of the effects

---

[1] Chapter 2 outlines these studies in detail.

of candidate positions and actions on voter evaluations (e.g., McGraw, 2011). Because I seek to study the differing effects of promises and non-promise policy positions, a survey experiment using hypothetical candidate speech provides the best course of action.

The first necessary stipulation is clarification of the trade-offs between internal and external validity that experiments provide, and emphasis on the critical utility found within survey experiments for this project. An experimental approach yields two important advantages, ultimately yielding strong internal validity so we can discern the specific effects of promises on voter behavior. First, this design allows me to carefully control each statement so that the level of ambiguity is exactly the same; no candidate will be further detailing their precise platform *except* by indicating that they will act on it in the future. Since I argue that these statements are used strategically, it would be difficult to cull enough data from statements actual candidates use. Throughout the remainder of the book, I craft statements that allow for careful distinctions between promise and non-promise states that also do not differentiate in ambiguity.[2] Second, using experiments allows for a more careful measurement of how statements effect evaluations of candidates. Using polls and survey data creates considerably more noise, which makes it difficult to know what drives results, if it is language, omitted variables, or race-specific events, including features of the particular candidates. Thus, executing a prospective study on promises that culls the effects of promises from real effects would yield a completely believable context and high external validity, but it would make measurement strategies incredibly difficult.

Although experiments remove voters from the precise conditions of a lived campaign context, I have taken care in all the studies I report in this book to create experimental designs that use appropriate contexts, similar to what voters may hear from real candidates (McDermott, 2011). And, while the candidate statements are relatively short (one sentence), many voter interactions with candidate and elected official speech occur through snippets on television, radio, and social media or quotations in print media, which the statements resemble. In the US context, an estimated 1 percent of the population receives their political information

---

[2] As discussed in Chapter 2, distinctions in ambiguity affect voter behavior as well. While voters may perceive promises and indications of commitment as similar to ambiguity because candidates indicate more or less information about the actions that they would take, promises are distinct from conceptions of ambiguity measured in other studies, because ambiguity focuses on specificity of platforms on issues.

directly from candidate speeches or the candidate's website or other promotional materials (Gottfried et al., 2016), compared to the shorter snippets of information that voters receive from news media. Thus, the statements I feature in my studies are similar to what voters would see in other contexts.

Further, in efforts to increase the reliability of the data gathered here, I sample from many different contexts over several studies to demonstrate how promises imply commitment and subsequently polarize voter evaluations of candidates. Some of the studies are given to student samples at a major research university, which, despite the non-representative sample, have been useful for studies on voter behavior (Druckman and Kam, 2011). Other experiments are deployed on the online convenience sample of Mechanical Turk, which tends to be more white, liberal, and educated, but useful for experiments that do not moderate on any of these qualities (Berinsky, Huber, and Lenz, 2012; Paolacci and Chandler, 2014; Levay, Freese, and Druckman, 2016). And still other studies (the most important) are given to participants in the YouGov panel (Rivers, 2008), which is the most representative sample. That the samples collected across the studies in this book give a strong narrative throughout the book is another test of the study validity and reliability of the results found here.

A second necessary stipulation is that experiments tend to narrow focus on a much smaller set of issues – or a single issue in my case – than actual candidate speech and opinion polls would, were I to cull data from them. While this comes with advantages and disadvantages, since this study attempts to provide empirical evidence of a theorized concept, starting with a single issue allows me to test the possibilities of promises and various aspects of the commitment process (Druckman and Leeper, 2012). This brings me to why I focus on gun control among the multitude of issues that I could use for these experiments.

First, study participants are likely to be conscious of gun control as an issue of public policy. Voters are aware of political stances, and voters are likely to have a stance on the issue. More importantly, there is likely to be equal representation of voters on both sides of the issue. In the 2012 American National Election Studies survey, about 45 percent of Americans wanted to increase gun control, 49 percent of Americans wanted to keep gun control the same, and about 6 percent wanted to decrease gun control (ANES, 2012). The Gallup poll in 2013 reports 49 percent of Americans want stricter gun control, 37 percent want to keep gun control the same, and 13 percent want less strict gun control (Gallup, 2014). Similarly, a Quinnipiac University poll asks respondents if they support or oppose gun control. It shows that 53 percent of respondents support stricter gun control, and 42 percent of respondents oppose stricter gun control in late March 2014 (Polling Report, 2014). Thus gun control will support strategic sampling. This will allow me to be strategic in moderating the sample based on respondent agreement with gun control. Since my theory rests on the notion that promises will motivate behavior differently based on voter–candidate alignment, finding an issue where there is a relatively even distribution of the population and therefore even sampling of voters who agree and disagree with the treatments makes it easier to test.

Second, voters are familiar with the issue because gun control is represented in candidate speeches. Both promise and non-promise policy statements are used by candidates to talk about the issue of gun control. This condition helps provide external validity to the experiment, as it means that statements subjects read will be similar to statements they will encounter in real settings. That candidates openly discuss gun control also makes the context of the candidate rhetoric more relevant to voters, and therefore the survey subjects. Candidates have mentioned gun control in the context of campaign promises over the course of several different elections. It was discussed generally in the presidential debates of 1976 and 2012 (Debate, 1976, 2012); in relation to the 1994 Brady Bill in 1996 (Debate, 1992); and in relation to self-protection, sports, and criminality in 2000 (Gore, 2000). It is also an issue where candidates make promise and non-promise statements, and sometimes in the same debate. For instance, during a televised debate in 2000, George W. Bush responded to a voter question about gun control without making a promise, saying, "I believe law-abiding citizens ought to be allowed to protect themselves and their families. I believe that we ought to keep guns out of the hands of people that shouldn't have them." That same debate, Al Gore responded to Bush's position with a promise "to not do anything to affect the rights of hunters or sportsmen" (Gore, 2000). Candidates also discuss gun control in primary election contexts, where candidates in the same party offer competing platforms and in general elections across party platforms. Public discourse also frequently addresses gun control.[3]

---

3 While I anticipate gun control will be a critical topic in US politics for some time, several visible events centered gun control as a matter of public discussion during data collection for this book. A movie theater shooting and an elementary school shooting in 2012 increased the prevalence of gun control discussions in America (The White House, 2013). Gabrielle Giffords's ensuing gun control campaign and the National Rifle Association responses helped keep the conversation alive for quite some time following her own attack and other public shootings (BBC, 2013; Keen, 2012).

At the same time, the fact that public policy on gun control rarely changes provides additional support. In fact, in the year much of the data for this book was fielded, only a handful of the many gun control bills presented in Congress and in state legislatures actually passed (Smart Gun Laws, 2014). Thus, in studying an issue that is difficult on which to change policy, I also create a difficult test for candidate rhetoric. If study participants do not expect change on the issue, rhetoric should matter less than if the policy has a greater chance of moving, thereby understating the impact of promises on voters.

In sum, the remaining data strategy of the book is to measure how the public understands promises and uses promises to evaluate candidates. The next step is to ascertain that the definition of promises I use, drawing from several fields, matches the understanding of how promises matter to voters. The following sections of this chapter introduce two studies that confirm the definition of promises as an indication of action *and* a way for candidates to signal an elevated commitment on an issue.

4.2 STUDY 1: THE PROMISE DEFINITION STUDY

The first study asks respondents to consider a variety of candidate statements, including promises and non-promises, and determine if the statements are promises. As both a proof of the concept of promises presented in Chapter 2 *and* to connect subsequent findings to variations in commitment, verifying this definitional distinction among voters is necessary. The data indicates that voters do perceive differences in the formation of candidate policy statements and do not consider all statements to be promises. Further, I demonstrate that the crafting of a promise does not depend on promissory language such as "promise," "guarantee," or "pledge."

4.2.1 Study Description

This study measures voter opinions of what types of candidate statements are promises and which are not by asking respondents to rate the level to which the respondent perceives candidate statements as promises. This rating task simply displays a randomly drawn candidate statement to each respondent who is asked to read the statement carefully. The respondent is then asked, "Is this statement a promise on gun control?" The answer choice is a sliding scale from 1, "Not at all," to 7, "Definitely." Because

TABLE 4.2 *Promise and non-promise statement types*

Statement Type	Promissory Language	Statement
Non-promise	No	I support increasing gun control.
Non-promise	No	I believe it makes sense to increase gun control.
Non-promise	No	I think it is a good idea to increase gun control.
Promise	No	I will work to increase gun control while in office.
Promise	No	If I am elected, my first task will be to increase gun control.
Promise	No	When I am elected, I will increase gun control in my district.
Promise	Yes	I promise that I will increase gun control.
Promise	Yes	I pledge to work to increase gun control.

there are so many candidate statements, each statement was displayed to respondents in a randomized order.[4]

A total of eight candidate statements were included in the study. Each statement was carefully crafted to easily classify it according to the binary scheme of promise or non-promise positions. That is, all promise position statements mention an action the candidate will take if elected. All non-promise statements mention the same position (in favor of increased gun control) without specifying an action or outcome related to gun control. In addition to testing distinctions between promise and non-promise statements, I also use this exercise to test whether simply using promissory language – e.g., promise, pledge, guarantee, assure, etc. – to signal a promise makes the difference in voters' minds or whether signaling an action or outcome that the candidate will work on when elected also affects voters' perceptions. As such, three of the statements were non-promise statements, three of the statements were promise statements without promissory language, and two of the statements were promise statements made using promissory language. The complete list of statements, and the type of the statement is listed in Table 4.2. The rating tasks essentially boil down into two groups: promises and non-promises.

---

4 I also use this opportunity to test if subjects find these statements similar to real statements candidates have made. I find that no statements are viewed as more plausible than any other statement and that all statements are rated as realistic. These results are in the Appendix.

After looking at these basic distinctions, I look at differences between promises with promissory language and promises without promissory language.

Based on my definition of promises, I anticipate that on average, respondents will rate promise statements as more of a promise than non-promise statements. I also anticipate that the mean ranking of all promise statements will exceed the midpoint (0.5), while the mean ranking of non-promise statements should fall below the mid-point. Finally, I anticipate that promissory language should have a minimal effect on responses. It is possible that attaching promissory language has a small positive effect, but I anticipate that the difference between statements made with promissory language and without promissory language is minimal. The underpinnings of the definition of promises used in this book require the candidate make a statement about an action or outcome, not to use promissory language.

4.2.2 Results

The promise definition study was fielded on Amazon's Mechanical Turk in November 2014 to 249 respondents. Mechanical Turk samples are convenience samples and not representative of the American public, but research has indicated that results are consistent with what we would expect from a representative sample. (See Berinsky, Huber, and Lenz (2012); Paolacci and Chandler (2014); Mullinix et al. (2015).) To analyze the data, I collapse the ratings of the statements into three groups: non-promise, promises without promissory language, and promises with promissory language. (Though each category follows the same pattern I describe below.) I then take the mean of the respondent ratings and compare across the different groups. For ease of interpretation, I also rescaled the responses between 0 and 1, such that 0 indicates the respondent thought that the statement was not a promise and 1 indicated that the statement completely resembled a promise. The results are displayed in Figure 4.1.

A rating below the midpoint (0.5) indicates that the statement is not at all a promise, and a rating above the midpoint indicates that the statement can be perceived as a promise. The average rating for the non-promise statements ($\mu = 0.32$) was significantly lower than that of either promise statement ($\mu_{promissory} = 0.68$, $p < 0.001$; $\mu_{nonpromissory} = 0.72$, $p < 0.001$). Respondents did not distinguish between promise statements based on whether or not they included promissory language ($p = 0.23$).

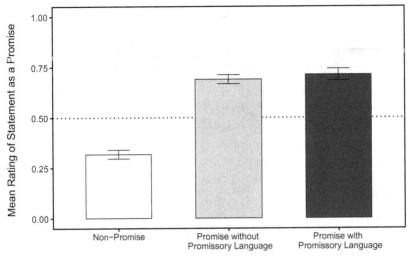

FIGURE 4.1 Respondent ratings of the candidate statements

Note: This graph reports the mean rating of respondents of how much the candidate statement resembles a promise. The error bar shows the 95% confidence interval around the mean.

Consistent with my definitions, respondents rated the non-promise statements as non-promises and both types of promise statements as promises, past the halfway point. This means that the proposed definitions of promises are consistent with voter assessments: policy statements incorporating proposed actions are considered promises while policy statements lacking proposed actions are not considered promises (confirming my hypothesis that promises are viewed as higher than the midpoint, and non-promises are viewed as lower than the midpoint). Additionally, as expected, these results indicate that promise statements do not require promissory language. Indeed, there is no significant difference in ratings between the promise statements without promissory language and the promise statements with promissory language. This means that the aspect of candidate statements that reflect whether a promise is being made is the portion of the statement that reflects potential action.

Ultimately, these results indicate that my definition of promises is consistent with how voters view promises. The respondents who were not given the proposed definition of a campaign promise prior to the study identify the same statements as promises as the proposed definition here. At the very least, these findings indicate that promises are more than simply a description of a candidate's position.

4.3 STUDY 2: PROMISES AND COMMITMENT

The second goal of this chapter is to demonstrate that promises are associated with greater levels of commitment to the policies to which they are attached. Study 2 uses a similar measurement technique as Study 1, but this time I investigate how the different statements affect ratings of commitment and effectiveness. I demonstrate not only that the public differentiates between types of statements in a way that reconciles with the proposed definition or promises but that promises also induce greater expectations of commitment to the attached issue. That promises correspond to greater levels of commitment matches my assertions in Chapter 2.

4.3.1 Study Description

As in the previous study, I presented respondents with a candidate statement and then asked them to consider how that statement reflects commitment. I used the same statements detailed in the previous section. Here, I also included a neutral statement on gun control where the candidate simply says, "Gun control is a difficult issue." This produces three groups of interest for this experiment: promises made with promissory language, promises made without promissory language, non-promise statements on gun control, and a generic statement made without a position on gun control.

I then investigated connections between the statements and respondent assessments through two questions. First, I asked, "How committed do you think the candidate is?" Responses were on a 5-point scale with lower numbers indicating "Not committed" and higher numbers indicating "Very Committed." The second question further considered levels of commitment by considering how much effort the candidate might exert on that policy issue. I asked, "How effective do you think the candidate will be on gun control policy?" This question used a 5-point response scale with lower numbers indicating the candidate was "Not Effective at all" and higher numbers indicating that the candidate was "Extremely effective." The results were transformed to a 0–1 scale for consistency and ease of interpreting the results.

As I argued before, my theory proposes that promises should be linked to higher levels of commitment and higher expectations that candidates will work toward the political goals in question. For this experiment, then, I anticipate that promises – with and without promissory representation – should induce higher expectations of commitment and effectiveness for candidates than statements made without promises or without any position at all. The relationship between non-promise statements and non-position statements is somewhat less clear from the main tenets of my theory. However, while policy statements may lack a promise, non-promise statements still cause the candidates to take a position on gun control, and voters may consider them evidence that a candidate is more committed and effective than a candidate who does not take a position on the issue at all.

4.3.2 Results

This study was fielded to 568 students at a major research university as an online survey in November 2016, February 2017, and April 2017. Although this is not a representative sample of US voters, Druckman and Kam (2011) indicate data relying on such samples can still be informative if analyzing experimental outcomes, as long as student status does not affect the treatment. Although students are relatively new to voting, they are not new to political participation. And, while college students may be less engaged in the political process than average, data indicates that students in 2016 were more politically engaged than in previous years (Zinshteyn, 2016). Regardless of participation, by the time they attend college, most students should be familiar with US democracy and be able to form opinions about campaign promises.

Figure 4.2 shows the results for respondent assessments of candidate commitment based on promise. Candidates rated as having the most commitment to gun control are those who made promises with promissory language ($\mu = 0.75$). These candidates are rated as being significantly more committed to gun control than candidates who made promises without promissory language ($\mu = 0.65$, $p < 0.001$). The next highest rated group, those who saw candidates with non-promise statements, falls below the midpoint of the scale where candidates might even be perceived as having significant commitment ($\mu = 0.38$). And the difference between promises without promissory language is much larger than the difference between promises without promissory language and non-promise statements ($p < 0.001$). All candidates taking a position are rated significantly more committed to gun control than the neutral candidate who only said that gun control was an important issue.

While the means are generally slightly smaller, the results for assessments of candidate effectiveness are quite similar to those of candidate commitment. Figure 4.3 displays the data. Again, the ratings of

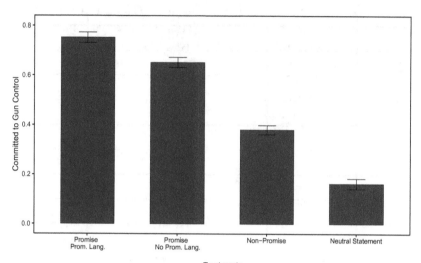

FIGURE 4.2 Candidate commitment

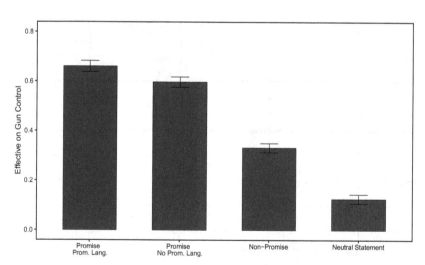

FIGURE 4.3 Candidate effectiveness

Note: These graphs report the mean rating of respondents for candidate commitment and efficacy conveyed through statements about gun control. The 5-point scale has been transformed to fit on a 0 to 1 scale so that the difference in means can be interpreted as a percentage change induced by treatment. The error bar shows the 95% confidence interval around the mean.

candidate effectiveness decrease from promises to non-promises to the neutral statement. There is also a small and significant difference between promises with and without promissory language, with promises with promissory language rated slightly higher ($\mu_{change} = 0.07, p < 0.001$). This difference is substantially smaller than the difference between promises (without promissory language) and non-promises ($\mu_{change} = 0.27, p < 0.001$).

The results indicate three important conclusions. First, the level of projected commitment to gun control decreases from promises to non-promises to the neutral statement. This means that voters perceive any position on the issue as increasing a candidate's commitment to that issue over no statement at all. However, promises increase the perceived commitment of the candidate to the issue the most. The replicated finding when measuring increases in perceived effectiveness provides further support. That voters perceive a distinction in levels of commitment by the degree that candidates are willing to specify a position at all and then say they will act on it underscores the notion that promises are useful tools in suggesting how well candidates will represent their constituents. Second, unlike in the last study, promises made with promissory language caused the candidates to be perceived as slightly more committed. While this suggests that promissory language may have a role in establishing commitment, this difference was quite small. That promises made without promissory language are still rated as demonstrating commitment and effectiveness at a greater level than a statement without a promise is further proof that this concept is not simply about using promissory words but more about describing post-election actions or outcomes.

4.4 CONCLUSION

The primary goal of this chapter is to examine whether voters conceive promises as theorized in Chapter 2. In demonstrating that they do, I argue that the most effective way to investigate the affect of promises on voter behavior is to use experiments to test for the effects of campaign promises since it is nearly impossible to separate the effects of promises from campaign-specific effects that exist in observational data. Candidates have varied backgrounds, experience, and personalities and come to the table with partisan and demographic differences;

they also make a plethora of statements on many different issues that might affect constituents differently and would be impossible to control for (Iyengar et al., 2008). However, experimentation allows me to isolate how promises matter, and experiments described in subsequent chapters will include additional pieces of information to determine how promises matter in the presence of external factors and matter because of them.

I also illustrate why gun control is a particularly useful topic on which to experiment about gun control. Choosing gun control was a strategic decision that makes sampling more feasible. Because gun control boasts a relatively even distribution of support among the population, I leverage this in later studies where I need to divide the sample based on agreement with gun control. Second, gun control is a topic commonly discussed over multiple elections, which means that the statements provided here have contextual validity. In sum, for this chapter and all subsequent chapters in the book, experimentation on gun control is the best mode of measurement.

Perhaps most importantly, this chapter demonstrates that voters agree with my definition of promises and recognize a heightened sense of commitment in candidates who make them. This chapter uses two studies featuring these types of tests to examine the internal validity of the distinction between promises and non-promise positions. Respondents indicate they recognize important and meaningful distinctions between promises and non-promises. The first study underlines that promises are linked to statements of action. And, while promissory language slightly elevates the identification of promises, it is sufficient for candidates to indicate action on an issue with no promissory language for a statement to be considered a promise. The second study underscores a key component of how promises matter, according to my theory: Promises are linked to increased perceptions of commitment and effectiveness on the issue in which they are made. Together, these data unambiguously link promises to statements including action and, in turn, heightened expectations of commitment and effectiveness by candidates. These studies open the framework to demonstrate that not only do voters recognize promises, they recognize a variation in how committed candidates are with respect to promises. It follows that these statements would then have downstream affects on voter decision-making and assessments of candidates. The next several chapters investigate this possibility.

APPENDIX

4.A Mechanical Turk Sample

The sample from Study 1 was recruited from Amazon's Mechanical Turk in November 2014. The study recruited 249 US adults. A basic demographic profile for respondents is found in Table 4.3.

4.B Candidate Statements as Realistic

Respondents were asked, on a 7-point scale, whether they found the same candidate statements to be realistic or not. Figure 4.4 displays these results. The scale has been transformed to a 0–1 scale such that 0 indicates the statements were found to not be realistic at all and 1 indicates that the statements were completely realistic. On the whole, respondents found the candidate statements to be realistic or above the midpoint of 0.5, and all were significantly higher than that point. Respondents found promise statements without promissory language to be most realistic ($\mu = 0.71$) and rated significantly more realistic than promises without promissory language ($\mu = 0.67, p = 0.02$) and non-promises ($\mu = 0.67, p = 0.005$). These statements are most represented in recent debates as shown in Chapter 3. Promises made with promissory language were indistinguishable from non-promises ($p = 0.87$). On the whole, however, these differences are substantively small. These results give some support that the statements chosen were viewed as realistic on the whole.

TABLE 4.3 *Mechanical Turk sample demographics*

	Minimum	Maximum	Mean	Std. Error	N
Male	0	1	0.38	0.03	249
White	0	1	0.72	0.03	249
Age	18	70	33.35	0.73	249
Party identification	−1	1	0.32	0.04	228
Education	1	6	3.88	0.08	249
Registered voter	0	1	0.82	0.02	249

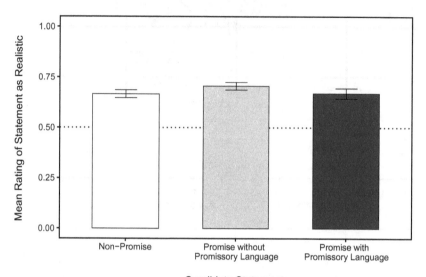

Candidate Statements

FIGURE 4.4 Candidate statements viewed as realistic

Note: This graph reports the mean rating of respondents of how much the candidate statement resembles a promise. The error bar shows the 95% confidence interval around the mean.

TABLE 4.4 *Student sample demographics*

	Minimum	Maximum	Mean	Std. Error	N
White	0	1	0.53	0.02	553
Male	0	1	0.41	0.02	553
Age	18	26	19.26	0.06	445
Party identification	−1	1	−0.30	0.02	553
Registered voter	0	1	0.97	0.01	431
Interest in news	0	1	0.82	0.01	467

4.C Student Sample

The sample from Study 2 was recruited from a student sample in a political behavior laboratory at a major research university. The study was conducted in two separate collections: one in November 2016 and the other in February 2017. Because the questions were the same in both waves, responses were combined in a single report. The study recruited 553 young adults (between the ages of 18 and 26). A basic demographic profile for respondents is found in Table 4.4.

PART III

THE EFFECT OF PROMISES
ON VOTER BEHAVIOR

5

How Promises Polarize Voters

Part I of this book introduced the concept of promises, and the theory of how promises heighten perceptions of candidate commitment to issues and thereby change voter evaluation of candidates. Part II of the book demonstrated that issue positions vary by whether they incorporate promises or not, and that voters recognize variations in issue positions. In Part III, I investigate how promises influence voter evaluation of candidates. I begin by examining how campaign promises influence evaluations prospectively. In this chapter, I further test the link between promises and vote choice by experimentally examining how promises affect voter support of candidates. In particular, I examine how promises shape perspectives on commitment and character to influence vote choice.

As I argue in Chapter 2, a promise signals stronger commitment to an issue than non-promised statements, and in turn, that signal of higher commitment indicates that the candidate will be more likely to follow through on that issue. Voters prefer candidates who both take positions similar to the voters' (Downs, 1965[1957]) and are more likely to create change closer to the voters' preferred policies (Rabinowitz and Macdonald, 1989). By signaling greater commitment, a candidate assures a voter of her intent to act while reducing voter uncertainty (Alvarez, 1997). Accordingly, I hypothesize that promises – more than non-promise statements – polarize voter opinions on a candidate: Voters will prefer promises on stances with which they agree and will be less favorable to promises on stances with which they disagree. (Table 5.1 contains the full set of hypotheses tested by the two studies in this chapter, and displays which study tests which hypothesis.) One important question

TABLE 5.1 *List of hypotheses and experiments*

Hypothesis	Study 1: Single Candidate Experiment	Study 2: Paired Candidate Experiment
Promises polarize voter opinions		
(1) Voters who agree with a candidate prefer a candidate who promises on that issue.	X	X
(2) Voters who disagree with a candidate prefer a candidate who does not promise on that issue.	X	X
Promises change expectations for follow-through		
(3) Voters expect candidates who promise to be more likely to follow through than candidates who do not promise, regardless of candidate or voter position.		X
Promises change character evaluations		
(4) Promising increases voter expectations of honesty.		X
(5) Voters view promisers as less open-minded than non-promisers.		X

Note: This table enumerates and summarizes a list of hypotheses fully argued in Chapter 2, and depicts which study tests which of the hypotheses.

I ask in this chapter is how voters distinguish between expectations of candidates' action on an issue and expectations for how policy might change. As I argue here, voters' assessments of candidate character, which promises tend to shift, may be crucial.

To examine the effects of promises on voter decision-making, I present the results of two survey experiments. One experiment, fielded to a convenience sample, examines promises using statements by a single candidate. The second experiment, fielded to a nationally representative sample, features a pair of candidates making different statements about gun control. (Table 5.1 also maps which study tests which hypotheses.) Using these data, I demonstrate that promises affect voter evaluations of candidates. Promises largely seem to polarize voter opinions on candidates, typically making supporters of a position more strongly support promisers, but can also be neutral. Promises also cause opponents of a position to more strongly oppose promisers. Ultimately, I find that the effects of promises are asymmetric: The negative effects of promises tend to be greater than the positive effects.

I also investigate how promises might affect voter evaluations. First, I hypothesized that promises should elevate voter expectations of candidate follow-through such that candidates who promise are seen as more committed to the issue and more likely to actualize the positions that they take into realized policy. This hypothesis corresponds to the argument that promises polarize voters based on issue agreement. If voters expect candidates to be more likely to follow through on their positions, they would prefer someone taking the opposing stance to be less committed to that issue and less likely to produce policy on that issue. Second, promises should also affect how voters perceive candidate character. As Kinder (1986) has demonstrated, voter opinions of candidate character are also important to perceptions of favorability. I hypothesized that promising could make candidates appear more honest and trustworthy, as a promise reveals more about intentions and interests. This means that voters would perceive promises as positive regardless of agreement. However, promising could also make voters suspicious about candidate intentions. On measures of follow-through and honesty, it was demonstrated in Chapter 2 that voters might be skeptical of candidates' ability to follow through on promises or that promises might cause voters to think candidates more dishonest because they believe candidates act only to garner votes rather than out of any sincere commitment (McGraw, Lodge, and Jones, 2002). I also suggest that promises might decrease voters' belief in candidates' open-mindedness. The experiment shows that promises not only decrease perceptions of open-mindedness but also make candidates appear less honest as well as less open-minded. That promising has a mixed effect on attitude formation seems to match narratives about voter skepticism over promises (Mansergh and Thomson, 2007). The mixed effects may help explain the asymmetric finding above. That the negative opinions among voters who disagree with a promiser are stronger than the positive affects among those who agree may be tied to how promises increase appearances of commitment but decrease ratings of candidate character.

5.1 STUDY 1: PROMISES AND VOTE CHOICE

Voters clearly differentiate between whether candidate positions are promises or not. This study further tests whether voters both differentiate between promises and non-promises and make decisions differently based on that distinction. As a result, it provides tangible evidence that promises affect candidate evaluations, and in a nuanced way. It confirms some of the basic tenets of my theory, such as that promises typically attract like-minded voters more strongly than statements made without a promise, though I also find that promises can also have little impact on voters who agree. Also, promises can repel different-minded voters more strongly than non-promises.

5.1.1 Design

This study portrayed a hypothetical candidate, manipulating whether or not they promise and their position on gun control to determine how both candidate position and promises affect voters' support of candidates. The study involved three parts: measurement of the respondent's position on gun control, the experimental treatment (a 2 × 2 design), and finally, measurement of candidate support.

First, respondent positions on gun control were measured to establish agreement or disagreement with the hypothetical candidate a priori. Respondents were asked to indicate if they "favor" or "oppose" stricter gun control. The question was formulated this way (instead of the ANES version, which distinguishes between those who oppose and those who want to lower barriers for gun ownership) for strategic reasons: In most public polls, about half of the respondents prefer stricter gun control, while the other half oppose stricter gun control (Polling Report, 2014). Generally, less than 10 percent favor making gun control less stringent (ANES, 2012), and it would be difficult to effectively sample that group without excessively large sample sizes. As such, for the purposes of this (and the remaining studies), I have opted to group all individuals who oppose stricter gun control together.

Next, respondents received the treatment: a vignette about a hypothetical candidate who makes a statement about gun control to voters. Candidate profiles involved two important pieces of information that were independently randomized: candidate position on gun control and statement type i.e., whether the candidate promised or not. Each candidate profile contained the same introductory text, which said,

A candidate (who will remain anonymous) is running in a local election. The candidate has spent the past several years in public service and is relatively well known to voters. The candidate has made several statements about policy. One of these statements is about gun control, and reads: [*randomized statement*].

The treatments, candidate position and statement type, were included in the second portion of the statement. Candidate position was created to match how respondent positions on gun control were laid out. Thus, candidates took one of two positions on gun control, either supporting stricter gun control or opposing stricter gun control. Candidate statements were also crafted by statement type so they could be attached to a promise or a non-promise statement. For example, candidates could say "I promise to increase gun control" or "I favor increasing gun control." Statements were carefully designed so that levels of specificity and ambiguity were all kept the same, as these factors affect voter behavior (see Tomz and Houweling, 2009). No candidates spoke about how they would implement their position. One candidate also served as a neutral control for this experiment. This candidate spoke neutrally (and vaguely) about gun control, saying, "Gun control is a difficult issue."

The statements in this study closely resemble those found in Chapter 4 and Study 2 in this chapter. Table 5.3 in the Appendix provides the full set of statements. Respondents were then asked about whether they would support or oppose that candidate (a 4-point scale ranging from "Strong Support" to "Strongly Oppose"), and how likely they would be to vote for a similar candidate (a 7-point scale ranging from "Extremely likely" to "Extremely unlikely"). (The full questionnaire is also in the Appendix.)

Ultimately, there are ten possible groups of respondents in this study because there are two different candidate positions (stricter, not stricter), two statement types (promise, non-promise), and a neutral candidate. All statements where respondents agree with the candidate should induce greater levels of support and votes than neutral candidates, and levels of support for neutral candidates should be higher than those whose positions differ from the respondents. For respondents who agree with the candidate position, levels of support for promisers should increase on average. In contrast, levels of support for promisers in groups who

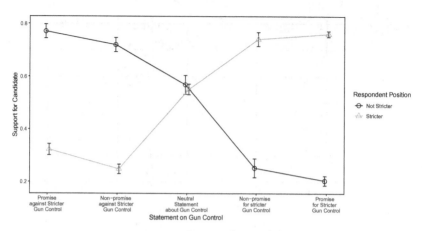

FIGURE 5.1 Support for candidate

disagree with the candidates should show a mean decrease. My theory makes no predictions about differences in these trends whether candidates take positions favoring or opposing stricter gun control.

5.1.2 Results

The Single Candidate Experiment was embedded in a survey that was fielded to 1,033 respondents on Amazon's Mechanical Turk in April 2017 using the Qualtrics survey platform. Since Amazon's Mechanical Turk is a convenience sample, demographics are not representative of the American public. However, Mechanical Turk is an acceptable sample for experimentation, providing that the demographics are not a key factor in the experimental design. (See Berinsky, Huber, and Lenz (2012) and Paolacci, Chandler, and Ipeirotis (2010).) The Appendix to this chapter provides demographic information and balance tests.[1]

More than two-thirds, 67.0 percent, of the sample favor stricter gun control while 33.0 percent oppose it. Figure 5.1 displays the results for respondent support of candidates based on the candidate statement. (Figure 5.2 presents nearly identical results for a second dependent variable: likelihood to vote for the candidate.) The y-axis corresponds to

---

[1] All demographics were balanced between promisers and non-promisers for both agree and disagree groups, with the exception of race. That said, the overall results are the same with and without controlling for whether respondents are white or not.

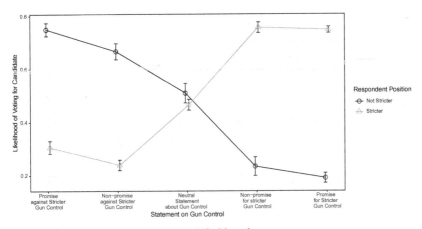

FIGURE 5.2 Likelihood to vote

Note: These graphs report the mean level of support and likelihood to vote for the candidates. Support is on a 4-point scale; likelihood to vote is on a 7-point scale. Both scales have been transformed to fit on a 0 to 1 scale so that the difference in means can be interpreted as a percentage change induced by treatment. The error bar shows the 95% confidence interval around the mean.

levels of support for a candidate, with higher values indicating support for that candidate, lower values indicating opposition to the candidate, and neither support nor opposition for the candidate in the middle. The x-axis features the candidate statements on gun control, ranging from a promise to maintain the status quo to neutral statements to a promise for stricter gun control. Finally, I present the results by the candidate's gun control position so that the darker line (with circles) represents respondents who oppose stricter gun control and the lighter line (with triangles) reflects respondents who favor stricter gun control. While I describe the results for candidate support here, the results are similar for both dependent variables.

First, notice that respondents who oppose stricter gun control have a decreasing level of support for candidates based on their statements on the issue. Among these, respondents who agreed with and saw candidates that also opposed stricter gun control prefer candidates who promise over candidates who do not promise ($\mu_{promise} = 0.77$, $\mu_{non-promise} = 0.72$, $p = 0.18$). And, those who disagreed with and saw candidates who favor stricter gun control prefer candidates who do not promise over those who do ($\mu_{promise} = 0.20$, $\mu_{non-promise} = 0.25$, $p = 0.23$). This means that respondents who oppose stricter gun control are most likely to support candidates who promise to oppose stricter gun control and least likely to support candidates who promise to favor stricter gun control.

Second, consider respondents who favor stricter gun control. Again, the line between mean values for respondents who saw candidates they agree with versus candidates with whom they disagree has a general positive slope. Among these respondents, those who agreed with and saw candidates that also favor stricter gun control do not necessarily prefer candidates who promise to those who do not ($\mu_{promise} = 0.76$, $\mu_{non\text{-}promise} = 0.74$, $p = 0.49$). Contradicting my theory's prediction, respondents in this group who saw and disagreed with candidates opposing stricter gun control prefer the promiser ($\mu_{promise} = 0.32$, $\mu_{non\text{-}promise} = 0.24$, $p = 0.01$).

These data nicely correspond to the predictions from my theory regarding the respondents who oppose stricter gun control. At the same time, among respondents favoring stricter gun control, the positive difference between the candidates promising stricter gun control and supporting stricter gun control is quite small, and not quite significant. So while promising to similarly minded candidates is not necessarily positive, it at least carries no actual penalty.[2] However, my theory incorrectly predicts the behavior of respondents who favor stricter gun control in this data collection. Those who disagree with the candidate prefer promisers to non-promisers. While I cannot conclusively explain this particular result with the current data set, I can propose two possible explanations. First, respondents might simply prefer promisers regardless of position. But this does not hold up to the data for the group in this sample who opposed stricter gun control. Second, there might be something unique about this experiment and these respondents, whether it is a slight variation in the treatment language, the timing of the experiment, or the sample from which the experiment was drawn. Since the next experiment confirms the theory for the groups, for now I will note that it seems likely the language of this particular candidate treatment produces this outlier result.

Despite the singularities for the group favoring gun control, this experiment highlights two important points. First, the experiment largely

---

[2] The next section explains why the benefit of promising to groups who agree with the candidate is so much smaller than the cost of promising to groups who disagree with the candidate. I argue this is largely because of differences in ratings of candidate follow-through and character.

confirms my theory that promises influence voter evaluations of candidates, which aligns with the larger narrative of this book. Second, promises do seem to have a polarizing effect on voter opinions – on one of the tested positions. Study 2 explores this effect in greater depth.

5.2 STUDY 2: PROMISES AND PATHWAYS

In this second study, I present the results of an experiment distributed through a nationally representative sample. This experiment features a paired candidate treatment, where respondents are asked to choose between two candidates, a promiser and a non-promiser. The design tests the basic tenets of the theory in this book by examining how voters evaluate promises relative to non-promise statements and how voter–candidate agreement on an issue changes how promises matter to voters. The experiment provides further evidence that promises polarize voters: Promises can make voters more likely to support candidates when voters agree with the candidate's position and not increase support when voters and candidates disagree. The Paired Candidate Experiment also tests how promises cause voters to differently evaluate candidate follow-through and character and demonstrates that promises change voter evaluations in part because promises change expectations of candidate commitment (or follow-through) and candidate character. First, I explain the design of the experiment and then present and discuss the main findings. I then examine the causal linkages between promises, candidate follow-through, and character, and conclude the discussion of the experiment by examining the potential of promises to shift electoral outcomes.

5.2.1 Design

The Paired Candidate Experiment involved three parts. First, I measured the respondent's position on gun control. Second, I presented the respondent with two candidate pairings. Each candidate pairing contained two different candidates, a promiser and a non-promiser, who held the same position on gun control. I asked the respondents to read each candidate's profile and select the candidate they preferred. Third, I followed up by asking the respondents about assessments of candidate follow-through and character.

I measured respondent opinion on gun control prior to my experiment using the two-response question format to again create two groups: respondents who favored stricter gun control and respondents

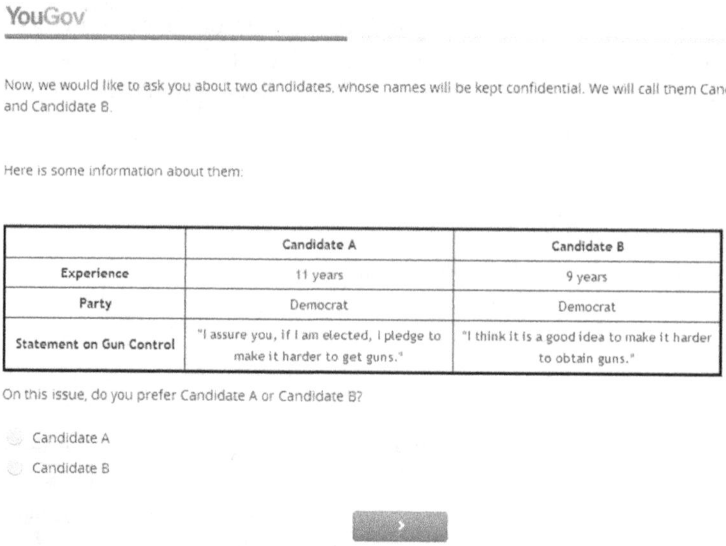

YouGov

Now, we would like to ask you about two candidates, whose names will be kept confidential. We will call them Candidate A and Candidate B.

Here is some information about them:

	Candidate A	Candidate B
Experience	11 years	9 years
Party	Democrat	Democrat
Statement on Gun Control	"I assure you, if I am elected, I pledge to make it harder to get guns."	"I think it is a good idea to make it harder to obtain guns."

On this issue, do you prefer Candidate A or Candidate B?

○ Candidate A

○ Candidate B

>

FIGURE 5.3 Example of candidate pairing

who opposed stricter gun control.[3] This experiment takes the form of a limited conjoint design. (See Hainmueller and Hopkins (2012) and Hainmueller, Hopkins, and Yamamoto (2014) for examples.) To measure opinions on gun control as before, I asked whether they "favor" or "oppose" stricter gun control.

The next screen gave respondents the treatment, a table of information about Candidate A and Candidate B, one who promises and one who does not. (See Figure 5.3 for a screenshot of how the question appears in the survey platform.) The first row of information contained the years of experience that each candidate has at the time. These values were drawn from the set $experience = \{7, 8, 9, 11\}$ randomly and without replacement. These levels of experience are chosen to be similar to each other so that this factor has a limited effect on respondent opinions, and to give the respondents some additional information about the candidate.

---

[3] As in the previous experiment, I refrain from using the three-choice question from the ANES because the percentage of people who want to decrease gun control is so small. I avoid having a candidate specifically appeal to this group because, without an impractically large sample, the category would not yield statistically reliable results.

In pretesting, none of these experience levels seemed to have a significant influence on respondent choices about the candidate.[4]

The last, and most important, row for this experiment contained a statement that the candidate makes on gun control. One of the candidates was randomly assigned a promise statement, while the other was randomly assigned a non-promise statement. Because the respondents saw multiple candidate pairings, I randomized the specific language of the candidates so that no respondent sees the same candidate or statement twice.[5] One promise statement was paired with one non-promise statement of the same position. For example, a positive promise statement was matched with one of the positive non-promise statements. The two candidates always agreed with each other's position on gun control, but whether the stance favored or opposed stricter gun control was randomly assigned.[6] If the candidates' party was specified, the candidates' positions on gun control was assigned randomly and independently of party, and the position does not always match the traditional position of the candidate's party. By holding position and party constant across candidates but independently assigning the different factors, I isolated the effects of promising from position and party preferences.[7] After viewing the candidate information, I asked the respondent which candidate was preferred.[8]

---

[4] About half of the respondents received a second row that contained information about the candidate's party. While party does not change the overall results of this experiment, it does introduce some interesting effects. I discuss the effects of party in Chapter 6.

[5] Table 5.6 in the Appendix lists the types of promise and non-promise statements that are possible.

[6] This randomization is the experimental manipulation. This design is a miniature version of a conjoint experiment (see Hainmueller, Hopkins, and Yamamoto (2014) and Hainmueller and Hopkins (2012)). Since I limit the conditions the respondent sees, the design is a limited conjoint design. Typically, a conjoint analysis will include several more categories of information, and several more types of pairings. Due to the time and length limitations of this survey, I was unable to include more information for the candidates or more candidate pairings per respondent.

[7] I would assume promising would not matter if positions were different since no respondent would prefer a candidate espousing a position they disagreed with, simply because that candidate promised.

[8] One critique of this design is that the treatment condition is too transparent. While it is true that respondents see both types of statements, they also see other information including candidate party and years of experience. It would take extremely good guessing for each respondent to know how statements looked in other treatments and the extent to which other respondents see different statements on gun control.

Finally, I measured two potential mediators of campaign promises, as proposed in Chapter 2. In particular, I assessed if the respondent differentiates between the two candidates in evaluations of expected follow-through, honesty, and open-mindedness, using these measures as mediators of the promise voting pathway. I presented the respondents with another comparison, asking respondents to choose the candidate that best fits the category in question. The first measure assessed perceptions of candidate commitment to the issue by measuring voters' perception of candidates' likelihood of following through on the issue. My theory predicts that voters will perceive promisers and non-promisers as equally likely to follow through on the issue. To measure whether this is the case immediately following the candidate pairing, I repeated the chart with candidate information for review. I then asked the respondent, "Which candidate is more likely to make gun control stricter?"[9] The options were "Candidate A is much more likely," "Candidate A is slightly more likely," "Candidate B is slightly more likely," and "Candidate B is much more likely."

The second set of mediators measured candidate character traits. I operationalized this metric by asking about candidate honesty and open-mindedness – two important measures of character that promises should affect. My theory predicts that voters will perceive promisers as more honest, though potentially less open-minded. After measuring expectations of candidate follow-through, I asked the respondent which candidate was more honest and, on a separate page, which was more open-minded. As before, the options ranged from "Candidate A is much more honest" and "Candidate A is much more open-minded" to "Candidate B is much more honest" and "Candidate B is much more open-minded." On each of these questions, the table with the candidate information was repeated in case the respondent needed to review either of the candidates' information.[10]

In order to increase the number of observations, I repeated the entire experiment with a second set of candidates, Candidates C and D, so that the respondents each received two candidate pairings, with four distinct

---

[9] Ideally, the respondents should be asked which candidate is more likely to follow through on their position. Because of a programming oversight, the respondents were asked the same question despite the candidates' specific stance on the issue. As I discuss later, this formulation might be confusing to respondents, and the effects for the "Less Strict" candidates are slightly smaller than findings for the "Stricter" candidates.

[10] The mediation questions were always listed in this order. While it is possible that order affected the outcome, I am doubtful it did. The mediators have the same general effect when they are all listed on the same page in Chapter 7. Thus, it is unlikely that the order of the mediator questions had a strong impact on the results in this chapter.

candidates. I chose the information for these candidates in a similar manner to the information selected for Candidates A and B.[11]

Ignoring the actual position the candidates can take on gun control, this experiment essentially produces two treatment groups: respondents who received candidate pairs with whom they agree and respondents who received candidate pairs with whom they disagree. For this experiment, the value of interest is the frequency with which promisers are preferred compared to the frequency that non-promisers are preferred. My theory produces the hypothesis that when voters agree with the candidate's position, voters should prefer promisers. Conversely, where voters and candidates disagree, candidates should prefer non-promisers. Because there are two positions candidates take, I examine two groups where candidates and respondents agree, and two where they disagree.

Unlike evaluations of candidates, voter expectations of candidate follow-through and assessments of candidate character should not depend on candidate–voter agreement. Voters should perceive candidates who promise as more likely to follow through and their statements as more honest, while assessing candidates who do not promise as more open-minded, as a lower commitment statement suggests greater willingness to consider new information about what considerations should drive policy.

5.2.2 Results: Promises Change Voter Opinions

The experiment was embedded in a omnibus survey fielded by YouGov in January 2014 to two samples of 1,000 American adults. YouGov randomly selects adults from their online panel of about 2 million people, using a selection algorithm to ensure that the respondents are representative of the general population by gender, age, race, education, party identification, ideology, and political interest. The organization estimates these figures from the 2010 American Community Survey and 2012 Current Population Survey.[12]

---

[11] There is some reason for concern about learning behavior among respondents. Indeed, results are slightly stronger among the second pairs of candidates than among the first. That said, all findings remain the same in both pairings, showing respondents learning how to take the survey do not solely drive the results.

[12] I use the unweighted data for my analysis because the treatments are randomly assigned independently of the weights, though the results do not change if I use the survey weights. See the Appendix for demographic variables and balance tests.

The sample is fairly evenly split on preferences for gun control. About 56.1 percent of respondents favored stricter gun control and 43.9 percent opposed stricter gun control. Since the candidates randomly favored and opposed stricter gun control, I have two treatment groups where the candidate and respondent positions agree and two groups where the candidate and respondent positions disagree.

The main hypotheses this experiment addresses concern the relationship between promises and vote choice.[13] Since the respondents are asked to choose between a non-promiser and a promiser, I present the effect of promising as whether the respondent preferred the promiser moderated by agreement. I then calculate the effect using an OLS regression of candidate choice and candidate promise. (This is described in detail in the Appendix.) A positive number indicates that the promiser is preferred to the candidate who takes the same position but does not promise. Conversely, a negative number indicates that a promiser is not preferred to the candidate who does not promise. Finally, a null result means that subjects did not distinguish between promise and non-promise statements.

Figure 5.4 presents the main test of this experiment.[14] Where the candidates and subjects agreed on the issue, they were viewed positively if they promised ($B_{favor} = 0.17$, $p < 0.001$; $B_{oppose} = 0.01$, $p = 0.064$). Where the candidates and subjects disagreed on the issue, they were viewed negatively if they promised ($B_{favor} = -0.27$, $p < 0.001$; $B_{oppose} = -0.64$, $p < 0.001$). The data supports my theory by indicating that promises tend to have a positive effect where respondents and candidates agree on stricter gun control and a null effect where candidates and respondents agree on not increasing gun control. Where candidates and respondents disagree, promises have a large negative effect, larger where candidates favor stricter gun control than where they oppose it. Still promising to those who disagree with you is still not preferred to not promising on the same stance. Except in the condition where candidates promise to maintain the status quo, the effect of promises is as predicted and a significant effect on respondent behavior. Based on agreement with respondents, however, promises seem to effectively polarize voter opinions about candidates based on candidate agreement.

---

[13] Tables for the regression results appear in the Appendix.
[14] The preference for the promising candidate in the second candidate pairing that each respondent received increases slightly. Removing the second pairing from my results does not change my conclusions, so I report the full set of results here.

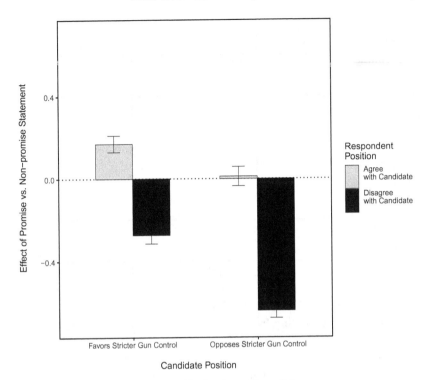

FIGURE 5.4 Evaluations of candidates

Note: This figure reports the effect of promises on preferences for the candidate, the β-value of the OLS regression of candidate choice and the binary variable promise. Both the candidate's position on gun control and whether the respondent agrees with the candidate or not moderate the effects. The error bar shows the 95% confidence interval around the mean.

These results show unexpected asymmetries my theory did not predict that make sense within the overall narrative and are important to understanding the functions of promises. First, the positive effect of promises is much larger and significant for candidates who favor stricter gun control, while the negative effect of promises is much larger for candidates who oppose stricter gun control. This could occur either because respondents who favor stricter gun control are more reactive to this issue or because a promise to not increase gun control or preserve the status quo affects individuals more negatively. Investigations of speech confirm that voters look more favorably at assertive language (Kronrod, Grinstein, and Wathieu, 2011), and they may perceive efforts to *change* a policy rather than *maintain* one as more assertive.

Negative effects of promising to voters who disagree with the candidate far exceed the positive (or null) effect of promising to voters who agree with candidates. This reflects, in part, the differences I find when evaluating expectations of follow-through and candidate traits as mediators. In fact, the asymmetry between potential benefits and potential costs of promising is great enough that it seems that promising should occur rarely, and only under particular circumstances. While my theory did not predict asymmetry, it fits well with what we know about human behavior, and the greater effects of negative stimuli compared to positive stimuli (Cobb and Kuklinski, 1997).

5.2.3 Why Promises Are Costly: Examining Causal Pathways

Having demonstrated that promises have a nuanced effect based on voter agreement, I consider a potential explanation for why promising might alter voter opinions of candidates. For this analysis, I estimate the mediating effects of expected candidate follow-through and assessments of candidate character following Imai and Yamamoto (2013) and Imai, Keele, and Yamamoto (2010). I first discuss the direct effects of promises on candidate follow-through and character, and then explain the effects of expectations of follow-through and character on candidate choice.[15]

There is a strong criticism of mediation analysis worth noting here. Bullock and Ha (2011) illustrate how the estimation of mediation pathways can be conflated with multiple mediators, and the importance of experimentally manipulating one mediator at a time. I am unable to fully separate and manipulate the mediators themselves with this experiment, both because the theoretical predictions do not lead me to predict different directional findings for follow-through and traits and because they do not allow for experimental manipulation of one construct without the other. The estimation of the mediators below might contain some bias. Nonetheless, the exercise points to several important findings in my data and contributes to my theory in conjunction with other direct tests of the mediators in other chapters.

Figure 5.5 displays how promise and non-promise statements affect expectations of candidate follow-through, moderated by candidate position and respondent agreement with that position. All respondents, regardless of agreement with the candidates' positions, believe the promising candidate is more likely to act on gun control if elected (for

---

[15] The Appendix to this chapter provides further details about the regression analysis and additional regression tables.

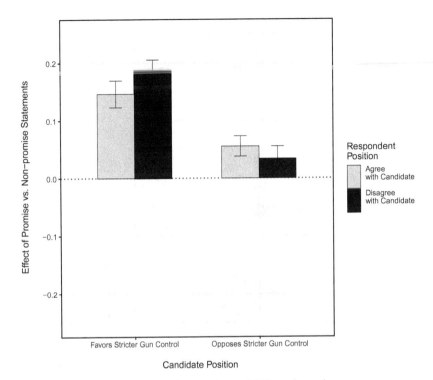

FIGURE 5.5 Expectations of follow-through

Note: This figure reports the effect of promises on anticipated candidate action, the β value of the OLS regression of candidate action and the binary variable promise. The effects have been moderated both by the candidate's position on gun control and by whether the respondent agrees with the candidate or not. The error bar shows the 95% confidence interval around the mean.

all groups, $p < 0.002$). There is a significantly larger effect among respondents who received a candidate who promised to increase gun control. This result helps explain the previous finding that negative reactions to promises are much larger than positive reactions and continues to support my theory: If individuals believe candidates who promise are more likely to act on an issue, overall preference for types of position statements should be polarized, much as they are in the main findings. Respondents who opposed stricter gun control preferred candidates who did not promise, while respondents who favored stricter control preferred candidates who did promise.

Now, consider how promises affected perceptions of candidate character. Figures 5.6a and 5.6b display the findings for assessments of candidate honesty and candidate open-mindedness. Surprisingly, regardless of the

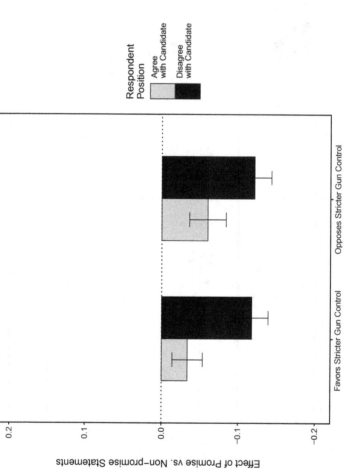

(a) Perceptions of Candidate Honesty

FIGURE 5.6 Assessments of candidate character

Note: These figures report the effect of promises on candidate honesty and candidate open-mindedness, respectively, and the binary variable promise. The effects have been moderated both by the candidate's position on gun control and

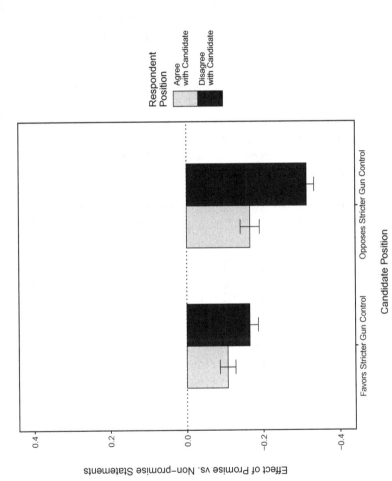

(b) Perceptions of Candidate Open-mindedness

FIGURE 5.6 (Continued)

candidate's position, respondents viewed the candidates who promised as less honest and less open-minded than the candidate who did not promise (for all groups, $p < 0.001$). While my theory indicates that assessments of candidate character might be positive, I also leveled some reservations: Voters are notoriously skeptical that candidates will keep their promises (Mansergh and Thomson, 2007). It seems that while voters do prefer promisers in some contexts, they have reservations about candidates who promise. Likewise, disagreement with the candidate's position had a greater impact on voters' belief in the candidate's honesty and open-mindedness than whether or not they promise. This finding may in part be influenced by projection, where individual beliefs on policy positions influence affect directed at candidates (Krosnick, 1988). Essentially, voters have positive affect toward candidates whose positions agree with their own and negative affect toward candidates whose positions disagree with their own, but preferences for like-minded candidates fail to erase the negative impact of voters' opinion about promises. The ultimate takeaway from this measure is that promises do induce negative inferences about candidate character among respondents of all positions.

While I discussed the possibility that promises might be viewed negatively in Chapter 2, I did not predict that assessments of candidate honesty would be opposed to predictions of candidate follow-through. While respondents view candidates who promise as more likely to follow through, they do not perceive those same candidates as more honest. My theory considered the possibility that both expectations of follow-through and perceptions of honesty would be negative because voters might perceive promises as pandering, but it is unexpected that follow-through would induce more positive expectations while perceptions of traits would induce more negative expectations. While independently these results make sense, that they would converge in the impact of promises is surprising. These items therefore seem to be measuring different aspects of a candidate: The correlation between the two measures is 0.05. And a principal component analysis confirms that while honesty and open-mindedness lay on quite similar components, honesty is completely orthogonal to expected follow-through. (See the Appendix online.) In short, this suggests that voters consider candidate traits quite differently than they do expectations for follow-through. These perceptions cannot be explained by agreement with the candidates as the above results indicate, but they may be explained by how promises shape voters' expectations. In part, while promises clearly change expectations about how candidates act in office, it seems they do not change expectations for policy outcomes in quite the same way.[16]

I now consider how promises might cause assessments of candidate follow-through and character might affect evaluations of candidates themselves – and potentially explain why promises have a larger negative effect on voters who disagree than positive or neutral effects among voters who agree. To determine the effect of these pathways on promising, I conduct a mediation analysis following Imai and Yamamoto (2013) and Imai, Keele, and Yamamoto (2010).[17] Because measures of candidate honesty and open-mindedness seem to function similarly for respondents, I average the two measures into *Traits* as a mediator along with *Follow-Through*. To further simplify the analysis, I also combine the candidate positions, moderating the sample only on whether respondents agree or disagree with the candidates' position. The algorithm for causal mediation requires independently regressing a measure of promises on vote choice, each mediator on promises, and then each mediator on vote choice to estimate the average causal mediated effects (ACMEs) of vote choice that operate through each mediators. Since these regressions yield the same pattern of results reported above, the regression tables used to compute for this analysis can be found in the Appendix.

The indirect effects of the mediators are listed in Table 5.2. Looking at the effects of the mediators, in each case, the ACMEs were statistically significant from 0. Corresponding to the data previously reported, the ACME for *Follow-Through* was positive in the *Agree* condition but negative for the *Disagree* condition. These data allow me to confirm that both *Follow-Through* and *Traits* are important in how promises matter to voters. Further, they help explain why the promising has a much larger negative effect among individuals who disagree. The ACMEs for *Traits* were negative across both conditions, while the ACMEs for *Follow-Through* were positive only in the *Agree* condition. In the Agree condition, the negative effect of *Traits* acts to suppress the positive effect of promises. In the Disagree condition, both the mediators have the same effect on candidate choice. The net result is that the negative assessments

---

[16] The Oversaturation Experiment in Chapter 6 continues to test the relationship between promises and expectations for follow-through and distinctions between follow-through and policy outcomes, demonstrating that this assertion seems to correspond with data.

[17] For this analysis, I used the Mediation package for R (Tingley et al., 2013).

TABLE 5.2 *Indirect effects of promising*

	Agree		Disagree	
	ACME	ACME/Total	ACME	ACME/Total
Follow-through	0.10* (0.08, 0.12)	0.71	−0.07* (−0.25, −0.19)	0.13
Traits	−0.12* (−0.15, −0.10)	−0.80	−0.22* (−0.25, −0.19)	0.42
Total	0.15* (0.10, 0.19)		−0.52* (−0.56, −0.48)	

Note: *This table reports the indirect effects as the change in percent in the outcome that the treatment produces through each mediator. The proportion of each indirect effect over the total effect is also presented. I estimated these effects using the Mediation package in R created by Tingley et al. (2013). Parameter uncertainty is estimated using quasi-Bayesian approximation with 1,000 simulations.* $*p < 0.01$.

of candidate character seem to suppress the positive gains from increased expectations of follow-through, resulting in an asymmetric effect for each condition.

This evidence confirms that both traits and expected candidate follow-through affect voter choice. And, it is through these mediators that promises affect candidate choice. These results also help to confirm that an asymmetric effect of promising between respondents who agree and disagree with the voters drives the moderated effect of expectations of candidate follow-through. The fact that a promise increases evaluations of a candidate's likelihood to follow through while causing the voters to think more poorly of the candidate creates an unbalanced main effect. Where candidates and respondents agree, candidate follow-through and candidate traits work in opposition to each other, reducing the overall effect of candidate traits. Where candidates and respondents disagree, candidate follow-through and candidate traits work together to produce a strong net negative effect. As I have argued, it follows that increasing the likelihood for promises would divide individuals based on their agreement with the candidate. Since promises have a negative effect on candidate character, this would serve to depress the positive effects of promising where respondents agreed with the candidate and further decrease the negative effects of promising where candidates disagreed with the respondent.

5.2.4 Candidates and Strategy

Finally, it is important to consider the implications of these findings for campaigns and election outcomes. To simulate these results from this experiment, I can calculate the effect of promising by subtracting the percentage of respondents who preferred the non-promising candidate $(V(C_N))$ from the percentage of respondents who preferred the promiser $(V(C_P))$ to determine a candidate's net gain from promising (E_p). Here, I modify the calculation to represent different preferences for gun control, using n to represent the percentage of the population that prefers gun control:

$$E_p = nV(C_P) + (1 - n)V(C_N). \qquad (5.1)$$

Using the sample estimates for gun control preference that were obtained through this survey (56.1 percent were in favor of stricter gun control), I calculate the precise advantage that a candidate would gain in a district with this make-up by either promising or failing to promise. Candidates who advocate to strengthen gun control gain a 13-point advantage by not promising. On the other hand, candidates who oppose making gun control stricter stand to lose 5 points by promising.

To generally predict how gun control may matter for districts with different splits of preferences on gun control, I use the established preferences for candidates on gun control from the above survey experiment to determine the point separating candidates who prefer stricter gun control from candidates who do not prefer stricter gun control. Figures 5.6 and 5.7 depict the percentage of the vote the candidate can expect to receive by promising, depending on their stance on strengthening gun control. In each graph, the candidate who promises is depicted with a solid line, and the candidate who does not promise is represented with a dashed line. For candidates who prefer stricter gun control, if more than 61.7 percent of their constituents prefer gun control, a promise will help them more than hurt them. Candidates who do not prefer gun control stand to lose much more: They need to have a district with 98.3 percent agreeing with them in order to gain by promising on that issue. Ultimately, it seems that only candidates taking the stance of stricter gun control would likely find an opportune district in which to promise.[18]

---

[18] This also assumes gun control is the only issue voters are considering. Chapter 6 also considers the effect of promises in the context of multiple issues.

The Effect of Promises on Voter Behavior

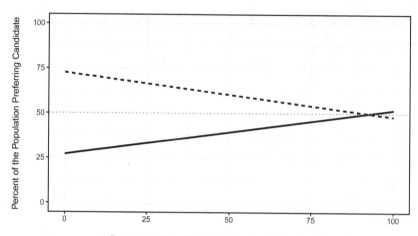

Percentage of the Population Favoring Stricter Gun Control

FIGURE 5.6 Projected candidate preferences based on district size: Candidates favor gun control

Note: This graph presents the projected level of support candidates would find in a district if they promised or not. The solid line represents the candidate who promises; the dashed line represents a candidate who does not.

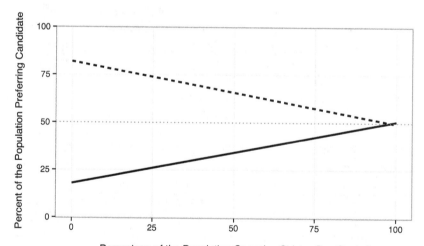

Percentage of the Population Opposing Stricter Gun Control

FIGURE 5.7 Projected candidate preferences based on district size: Candidates oppose gun control

Note: This graph presents the projected level of support candidates would find in a district if they promised or not. The solid line represents the candidate who promises; the dashed line represents a candidate who does not.

5.3 CONCLUSION

With the studies in this chapter, I intended to demonstrate that promises are distinguished from non-promise position statements when voters evaluate candidates. The survey experiments indicate that promises have an important and nuanced effect on voter behavior, and largely confirm the theory describing the prospective pathway in Chapter 2. However, some additional questions are worth considering.

First, promises can induce a small preference for candidates when the candidates and voters take a similar position. In some cases, voters who agree with the candidate's position are indifferent to promises.[19] And, promises decrease candidate favor among voters who disagree with them on gun control.[20] While my theory predicts this finding, it does not necessarily make a claim that one effect should be much larger than the other. I find here that the negative effect induced by promising is much larger than the positive effects of promising to constituents who agree with the candidate. This discrepancy in part seems to be explained by the mechanisms of promising.

My theory predicts that the effects of promising could be mediated by inducing changes in candidate commitment, measured here by changes in expectation for follow-through. Promises alter both expected follow-through and candidate character. While expectations for follow-through increased as the result of candidate promises, candidate character decreased. This finding is important because it helps explain how promises can work to help candidates; but in context of low voter expectations for the future, it seems like promises have a more nuanced effect on voter behavior than initially theorized.

---

[19] It is unclear when precisely promises are less useful. Inferences from Study 2 seem to indicate promises to maintain the status quo are less likely to appeal to voters. Study 1 and Study 2 together suggest that promises could have a null effect when made on issues counter to the party that is currently in power in Congress and the White House. Study 1 was fielded under Trump's presidency, when Republicans controlled both chambers of Congress and Study 2 was fielded under Obama's presidency, when Democrats controlled the Senate. Further work would be needed to separate these issues out. Nevertheless, promises have a much smaller positive effect than negative effect under either reasoning.

[20] In one case in Study 1, a promise was actually more positive than a non-promise when voters disagreed with the promising candidate's position. Given the three other cases in this chapter (and further cases in Chapter 6), it seems like this is a singular result perhaps driven by differences in samples or the way the experimental message was crafted.

Ultimately, this is a novel and important contribution. Many studies of position-taking and promissory representation consider promises and positions to be the same thing. This study, however, suggests an important takeaway for normative political science: Promises and non-promises are distinguishable by voters, not only because voters define them differently but also, and more importantly, because voters evaluate candidates differently based on the strength of the candidate position statements. As the studies presented here demonstrate, the statements induce important differences in how candidate commitment and character are evaluated as well.

Beyond the normative implications, this finding is important for those thinking about promises as well. Much of the work attempting to explain the "promise puzzle" – why voters expect officeholders to break promises they actually keep – focuses on understanding promise fulfillment and in what contexts rates of promise-keeping are kept (Naurin, 2014). But this chapter strongly suggests that researchers might find important answers in studying the prospective effects of promises as well, and in particularly thinking about how promises change voter beliefs around candidate follow-through and character, and how depending on voter agreement this changes candidate preference. While the goal here was not to explain the promise puzzle, the differences in how voters view promisers and non-promisers leave important suggestions for how researchers can continue to approach this problem.

While this chapter has demonstrated several important aspects of promises, there are also ways to vary the context in which promises are made. First, effects of promises might change when more circumstances are known to voters, including the candidate's party. Second, promises might have different effects in the presence of other promises. Chapter 6 investigates these possibilities and further examines the ways that promises might operate prospectively.

APPENDIX

5.A Study 1 Design and Sample

5.A.1 Study Design
The Single Candidate Study featured seven distinct candidate statements that were grouped by statement type. Because promissory language was

TABLE 5.3 *Promise and non-promise statements*

Statement Type	Promissory Language	Statement
Promise	Yes	I promise that I will not increase gun control.
Promise	No	I will work to prevent increase in gun control.
Non-promise	No	I oppose increase in gun control.
Neutral	No	Gun control is a difficult issue.
Non-promise	No	I support increasing gun control.
Promise	No	I will work to increase gun control while in office.
Promise	Yes	I promise that I will increase gun control.

demonstrated elsewhere to not change voter definitions of promises and because it would make group sizes small enough to lack explanatory power, I ignore variations in promissory language here. The full set of statements is listed in Table 5.3.

5.A.2 Study Sample

Balance is relatively even between treatment groups in every demographic category except race. Tables 5.4 and 5.5 display these results. In the agree groups, the non-promise treatment has slightly more white individuals (though not quite enough to achieve significance). The unbalance stems from the respondents favoring stricter gun control ($p = 0.19$) than from the candidates promising less strict gun control ($p = 0.94$). For the disagree group, there are significantly more white individuals in the non-promise group. Here, when looking at the specific positions, the in-balance falls more among respondents opposing stricter gun control ($p = 0.24$) than among respondents favoring stricter gun control ($p = 0.44$).

5.B Study 2 Design and Sample

5.B.1 Study Design

Table 5.6 shows the complete set of possible statements made by the candidates in Study 2. The statements were randomized so that each treatment included one candidate that promised and one candidate

TABLE 5.4 *Demographic and balance table: Respondents agreeing with candidate position*

	Promise		No Promise		
	Mean	N	Mean	N	*p*-value
White	0.81	151	0.74	325	0.12
Male	0.56	151	0.54	325	0.72
College degree	0.46	151	0.51	325	0.31
Voter	0.92	151	0.94	325	0.41
Political interest	0.71	151	0.69	325	0.43
Religious	0.60	151	0.61	325	0.83

TABLE 5.5 *Demographic and balance table: Respondents disagreeing with candidate position*

	Promise		No Promise		
	Mean	N	Mean	N	*p*-value
White	0.69	166	0.77	274	0.05
Male	0.55	166	0.59	274	0.34
College degree	0.48	166	0.49	274	0.89
Voter	0.92	166	0.91	274	0.91
Political interest	0.66	166	0.67	274	0.56
Religious	0.60	166	0.58	274	0.65

TABLE 5.6 *Candidate position statements*

Type	Position	Statements
Promise	Positive	I assure you, if I am elected, I pledge to make it harder to obtain guns.
	Negative	I assure you, if I am elected, I pledge not to make it harder to obtain guns.
	Positive	I give you my word, I promise that I will make it harder to get guns.
	Negative	I give you my word, I promise that I will not make it harder to get guns.
Non-promise	Positive	I think it is a good idea to make it harder to get guns.
	Negative	I think it is a bad idea to make it harder to get guns.
	Positive	I approve of making it harder to obtain guns.
	Negative	I do not approve of making it harder to obtain guns.

TABLE 5.7 *YouGov sample: Promise experiment*

Demographic	Minimum	Maximum	Mean	Std. Error
Age	19.00	93.00	47.73	0.38
Female	0.00	1.00	0.54	0.01
White	0.00	1.00	0.72	0.01
Married	1.00	6.00	2.79	0.04
Party	−3.00	3.00	−0.40	0.07
Ideology	−2.00	2.00	0.08	0.03
Employment	0.00	2.00	0.85	0.02
Education	1.00	6.00	3.23	0.03
Registered voter	0.00	1.00	0.99	0.00
Interest in news	1.00	7.00	1.88	0.03

that did not promise, but held the position constant between the two candidates. Further, because respondents saw two candidate pairs, the four candidates that the respondents saw all had different formulations of their specific stances so as to make the candidates feel as different as possible. Additionally, the endings of the sentences, "obtain guns" or "get guns" were randomized independently.

5.B.2 Sample
The demographic information for the survey respondents are presented here. Table 5.7 shows the demographics for the Paired Candidate Promise Experiment.

5.B.3 Mediation Calculations
For this analysis, I follow Hainmueller and Hopkins (2012) and Hainmueller, Hopkins, and Yamamoto (2014) in constructing a regression analysis of a conjoint data set. I transform the data as follows. The dependent variable, *Choice*, represents the average of the binary variable that is set to 1 if the candidate is preferred and 0 if the candidate is not preferred. I stack the data so that each observation is of one candidate.[21] The independent variable, *Promise*, is the binary variable that is set to 1 if the candidate promised and 0 otherwise. I also transform each

---

[21] Because the control variables are shared across observations, this artificially decreases the standard error because four observations come from one individual respondent. I analyze the regressions with cluster-robust standard errors to account for this.

of the mediators into a dummy variable with 1 indicating the chosen candidate.[22] This means the effect of promising can be calculated as follows:

$$Choice = \beta_0 + \beta_1 \cdot Promise \cdot E + e. \tag{5.2}$$

To calculate the ACME, I first model the effect of promise on the mediators in the *Vote Choice* model, where *trait* represents candidate traits and *Follow* represents candidate follow-through. With the factor variable *E*, I control for the candidate's level of experience for each observation. In this analysis, I measure the effect of promises on the mediators according to the following two equations. Because honesty and open-mindedness perform quite similarly to each other, I create an index of candidate character, *traits*.

$$Trait = \beta_0 + \beta_1 \cdot Promise + \beta_2 \cdot E + e, \tag{5.3}$$

$$Follow = \beta_3 + \beta_4 \cdot Promise + \beta_5 \cdot E + e. \tag{5.4}$$

I then measure the effect of promises on the dependent variable, *Choice*, while also including the mediators in the regression. The *Vote Choice* model is as follows:

$$Choice = \beta_6 + \beta_7 \cdot Promise + \beta_8 \cdot Follow + \beta_9 \cdot Trait + \beta_{10} \cdot E + e. \tag{5.5}$$

Finally, I use these values to estimate the indirect effect of promising on vote choice. As described by Imai and Yamamoto (2013), the algorithm predicts vote choice for the unobserved treatment values of the mediators. That is, if *M* represents the mediators, the algorithm first predicts *Choice* by setting *Promise* = 1 and *M* = *M*(0). The algorithm then predicts *Choice* by setting *Promise* = 0 and *M* = *M*(1). It computes the average difference between the two outcomes to estimate the ACME. Last, the algorithm estimates uncertainty through a non-parametric bootstrap procedure using 1000 Monte Carlo simulations, as detailed in Tingley et al. (2013).

The next step is to observe how the *Follow* and *Traits* mediate the impact of *Promise* on *Choice* in the *Vote Choice* Model. The results for

---

[22] Since *honest* and *open* are measuring essentially the same construct, and I proceed to create an index of candidate character, called *trait*, from an average of these two variables.

TABLE 5.8 *Candidate choice model where candidate and respondent agree*

	Dependent variable: Choice			
	(1)	(2)	(3)	(4)
Promise	0.146***	−0.007	0.298***	0.165***
	(0.035)	(0.031)	(0.027)	(0.026)
Experience = 7	0.047	0.040	0.017	0.017
	(0.043)	(0.038)	(0.034)	(0.032)
Experience = 8	−0.034	−0.025	−0.013	−0.011
	(0.033)	(0.028)	(0.026)	(0.024)
Experience = 9	0.006	−0.0004	0.017	0.011
	(0.016)	(0.014)	(0.013)	(0.012)
Follow-		0.501***		0.341***
through		(0.030)		(0.030)
Traits			0.686***	0.558***
			(0.029)	(0.034)
Constant	0.376***	0.212***	−0.039	−0.073**
	(0.036)	(0.033)	(0.032)	(0.029)
Observations	1,968	1,968	1,968	1,968
R^2	0.024	0.251	0.348	0.442
Adjusted R^2	0.018	0.246	0.343	0.438

Note: *This table reports the coefficient estimates of a Linear Probability Model with clustered standard errors in the parentheses. Controls for income, education, voting in the last election, gender, race, and attention to the news are included in the regression but not reported in the table. All results are unweighted.* $*p < 0.1; **p < 0.05; ***p < 0.01$

the regressions that measure the impact of the mediators on vote choice are found in Tables 5.8 and 5.9. Again, I have moderated the sample by whether or not the candidate and respondent agree or disagree. Here, each of the mediators is statistically significant in the presence of *Promise*. *Follow* has a positive effect in the *Agree* regressions and a negative effect in the *Disagree* regressions. *Traits* has a consistently positive effect in all regressions.

Including the mediators also has an interesting impact on the direct effect of *Promise*. Where candidates and respondents agree, primarily in the case of *Follow-Through*, the impact of *Promise* is indistinguishable from 0 in the *Agree* model. This means that for the *Agree* model, *Follow-Through* does mediate the interaction. In all other models, the

TABLE 5.9 *Candidate choice model where candidate and respondent disagree*

	Dependent variable: Choice			
	(1)	(2)	(3)	(4)
Promise	−0.521***	−0.434***	−0.285***	−0.232***
	(0.028)	(0.032)	(0.035)	(0.035)
Experience = 7	−0.028	−0.018	−0.018	−0.011
	(0.037)	(0.037)	(0.034)	(0.034)
Experience = 8	0.037	0.025	0.030	0.021
	(0.028)	(0.027)	(0.025)	(0.025)
Experience = 9	0.006	0.006	0.007	0.008
	(0.014)	(0.014)	(0.013)	(0.012)
Follow- through		−0.247***		−0.196***
		(0.032)		(0.028)
Traits			0.522***	0.487***
			(0.039)	(0.038)
Constant	0.738***	0.816***	0.346***	0.435***
	(0.033)	(0.032)	(0.044)	(0.044)
Observations	1,992	1,992	1,992	1,992
R^2	0.275	0.328	0.412	0.445
Adjusted R^2	0.270	0.324	0.408	0.441

Note: *This table reports the coefficient estimates of a Linear Probability Model with clustered standard errors in the parentheses. Controls for each model are included in the regression but not reported in the table. All results are unweighted.* $*p < 0.1$; $**p < 0.05$; $***p < 0.01$

coefficient of *Promise* increases, suggesting that *Traits* only partially mediates promises. In contrast, where the candidate and respondent disagree, *Traits* has a larger effect on reducing the coefficient of *Promise* than does *Follow-Through*. In these regressions, adding the mediators decreases the direct effect of promising in each case, suggesting that neither mediator fully mediates promises but both partially mediate *Promise*. In these regressions then, both *Follow-Through* and *Traits* appear to mediate a portion of the pathway from *Promise* to *Choice*.

For all groups, respondents expect the promiser to be more likely to follow through on their stated position than the non-promiser. Candidates promising on stricter gun control tend to be seen as more likely to follow

TABLE 5.10 *Effect of Promise on Mediators*

	Agree		Disagree	
	(Follow Through)	(Traits)	(Follow Through)	(Traits)
Promise	0.306***	−0.222***	0.353***	−0.452***
	(0.032)	(0.030)	(0.031)	(0.025)
Experience = 7	0.014	0.044	0.042	−0.019
	(0.042)	(0.036)	(0.041)	(0.031)
Experience = 8	−0.019	−0.031	−0.047	0.013
	(0.032)	(0.027)	(0.031)	(0.023)
Experience = 9	0.012	−0.017	0.003	−0.003
	(0.016)	(0.014)	(0.015)	(0.011)
Constant	0.329***	0.606***	0.319***	0.750***
	(0.034)	(0.031)	(0.036)	(0.028)
Observations	1,968	1,968	1,992	1,992
Adjusted R^2	0.090	0.062	0.122	0.285

Note: This table reports the coefficient estimates of a Linear Probability Model with clustered standard errors in the parentheses. Controls for income, education, voting in the last election, gender, race, and attention to the news are included in the regression but not reported in the table. All results are unweighted. *$p < 0.1$; **$p < 0.05$; ***$p < 0.01$

through than those promising to oppose stricter gun control. In contrast, respondents rate candidate character lower when the candidate promises, on both candidate honesty and candidate follow-through.

6

Further Testing the Effects of Promises

Chapter 5 established that promises affect voter behavior. This chapter examines the robustness of these effects when placed in conjunction with cues such as those that affect promise fulfillment. First, I repeat the Paired Candidate Experiment from Chapter 5, this time including partisan information. Then, I examine the impact of references to other issues. Chapter 5 established that promises have a neutral or small positive effect when voters agree with candidates but a large negative effect when voters disagree with candidates. The experiments in this chapter show that these effects are even stronger in the context of additional information, which is often the case in the real world of elections.

Table 6.1 summarizes the hypotheses discussed in this chapter. The first component I test is how partisan information affects reactions to promises. Party size, control of government, and differences in government models all affect whether officials fulfill their campaign promises (Mansergh and Thomson, 2007; Artes, 2011; Dimitrova and Kostadinova, 2013; Kostadinova, 2015; Håkansson and Naurin, 2016; Thomson et al., 2017), and it would make sense for partisan voters to react differently to promises based on changes in anticipated commitment that partisan information may supply (Naurin, 2011). The Paired Candidate Party Experiment repeats the Paired Candidate Experiment from Chapter 5 and includes partisan information for the candidates. This first experiment examines whether or not voters view statements that embrace the typical party position differently from promises that are made contrary to the party line. I discussed in Chapter 2 that voters may prefer promises made by members of their own party; promises that follow traditional party positions may appeal more to voters than those that do not, because in

TABLE 6.1 *List of hypotheses and experiments*

Hypothesis	Study Testing Hypothesis
(1) Voters will rate in-party candidate promises higher than out-party candidate promises.	Study 1: Party Experiment
(2) Promises along party lines will be preferred.	Study 1: Party Experiment
(3) Promises on more issues decreases the perception that a candidate will work more on the issue or realize the policy position proposed.	Study 2: Oversaturation Experiment

Note: This table enumerates and summarizes a list of hypotheses fully argued in Chapter 2, and depicts which study tests which of the hypotheses.

the former case, voters may be more inclined to believe the promisers will keep their promises. The results from the partisan experiment are slightly stronger than those without partisan information and indicate that voters prefer promises from co-partisans. However, in contrast to my expectations, candidates who make promises inconsistent with their party stance are preferred to those who toe the party line. Studies about promise fulfillment may explain voters' preference for candidates who defy party orthodoxy. Research has found that elected officials are actually more inclined to keep their promises if they are more similar to the other party's stances rather than similar to their own party's (Thomson et al., 2017; Kostadinova, 2013). Perhaps, voters recognize that promises that defy the party line are more prone to fulfillment, and therefore find them more appealing.

The results of the second study conformed to my expectations. The second experiment, the Oversaturation Experiment, further investigates the relationship between promising and commitments by examining the effect of candidate promises on voters in the presence of promises on other issues. This experiment also tests the relationship between whether promises change voter perceptions of candidate action or realized policy. As I anticipated, the results again demonstrate not only that promises do increase expectations that candidates will act in accordance with their promises but also that expectations for action are indeed higher than expectations for realized policy. While research has demonstrated that most of the public invests heavily in a small range of issues, candidates rarely focus solely on one campaign promise (Iyengar et al., 2008).

Thus, this Oversaturation Experiment represents a common phenomenon in the real world.

Overall, this chapter demonstrates two general lessons for how promises affect voter behavior. First, promises have an even stronger effect than presented in Chapter 5 when party information is included on candidate profiles. Second, even when partisan information and other issues are presented to voters, promises continue to matter the way my theory predicts. This provides evidence that the findings in Chapter 5 are robust to party information and in the presence of other issues.

6.1 STUDY 1: PAIRED CANDIDATE PARTISAN EXPERIMENT

A portion of the work on issue ownership considers how politicians act to reinforce it. For instance, Benoit (2004) investigates candidate attention to issues both in primary and general election debates, and shows that most candidates concentrate predominately on issues that are perceived to be addressed particularly well by their party – or issues that the party "owns" – in general elections, but they are more likely to mention issues the other party usually highlights in primary elections. Petrocik, Benoit, and Hansen (2003) note that the effects of issue ownership do not change significantly across media: In television advertisements as well as acceptance speeches, major party candidates stick to the script on their own issues. And, because candidate choice tends to be correlated with voter attention to issues, it appears that candidates who pay attention to their own issues have a strategic advantage over candidates who do not. This suggests that promises on party-aligned positions should be most attractive to co-partisan voters. However, candidates do sometimes make promises on issues their parties do not own (Brazeal and Benoit, 2001). Here, I test these possibilities by manipulating whether candidates promise against or along the party lines.

6.1.1 Design

To examine how including partisan information alters voter attitudes toward candidates, I leverage the experimental setup I used in Chapter 5 except that I include the candidate's party, in addition to candidate experience and a statement on gun control. As before, I first ask respondents about their preferences on gun control, then present the information and the statement about gun control, adding the candidate's party. Both the experience level and statements on gun control were assigned in the manner described in Chapter 5 so that each pairing displayed one candidate promising and the other not promising, but each taking the same position. For half of the respondents, the second row contained the candidate's party. The other half of respondents received no party information. The candidates' party was randomly assigned independently of the other rows in the table. Because I assume that respondents will be drawn to the name of the party over the strength of the statement as a result of increasing ideological sorting (Levendusky, 2009), each pair of candidates is given the exact same party information. This means that both candidates appear as Republicans or both candidates appear as Democrats.

If we ignore the precise partisan positions for now, the experiment formed a 2 × 3 set of treatments. Respondents could either agree or disagree with the candidate, and they either saw no party information, Republican candidates, or Democrat candidates. First, I use this information to determine whether voters prefer promises made by co-partisans to those made by out-partisans. Here, consistency refers to voter–candidate party alignment. Because politics is so fraught with party identification (Sniderman and Stiglitz, 2012), I anticipate that voters prefer co-partisans. By contrast, it is difficult to predict whether respondents will be more positive toward out-party candidates or candidates with no partisan information.

I also use this information to consider the impact of whether candidates are consistent with their party's issue alignment. Based on my formulation of commitment and policy statements, I anticipated that promises would further enhance candidate gains from highlighting issues their party is particularly well suited to address (Rosema, 2006), and we should see voters preferring co-partisan candidates over out-partisan candidates and candidates with no party assigned, holding agreement constant. That said, the reverse may be true as a greater level of commitment is necessary for candidates to convince voters with party-inconsistent issues (Brazeal and Benoit, 2001; Petrocik, Benoit, and Hansen, 2003). If so, promising against party lines may leverage a slight advantage for candidates.

6.1.2 Results

This experiment was fielded in January 2014 to two sets of 1,000 American adults through YouGov (see Chapter 5 for a description of YouGov's methodology). The sample had a greater number of respondents favoring

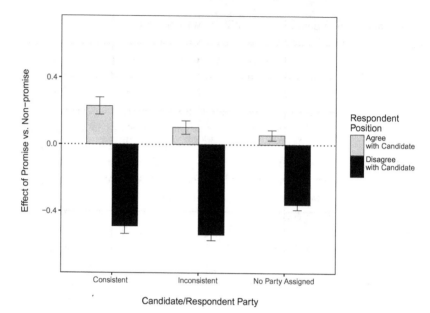

FIGURE 6.1   Effect of promising for co- and out-partisans

Note: This figure reports the effect of promises on candidate preference, the β value of the OLS regression of candidate choice and the binary variable promise. The effects have been moderated both by the consistency between candidate and respondent party, and by whether the respondent agrees with the candidate or not. The bar denotes the 95% confidence interval of the estimates.

stricter gun control (56.1 percent) than respondents opposing stricter gun control (43.9 percent). The sample was divided into the six groups described above, by candidate–respondent agreement and candidate–voter party alignment or issue–party consistency.

I examine first the effect of introducing party generally on the experiment results, and then I consider how party influences partisan and nonpartisan votes. Again, I consider the effect of promises as the difference between preference for the promiser and preference for the non-promiser. Figure 6.1 shows the effect of promising moderated by whether the respondents were given a candidate with the same party, different party, or no party at all. (For this exercise, pure independents were ignored and leaners were included with identified partisans.) First, the effect of promising is significantly larger for candidates promising to co-partisans, while there is no difference between candidates of a different party and nonpartisans. Respondents essentially prefer promising when both position and party align. Interestingly, candidates who made a promise with which the respondent disagreed suffered greater negative effects if their party affiliation was not assigned than if it was. However, respondents

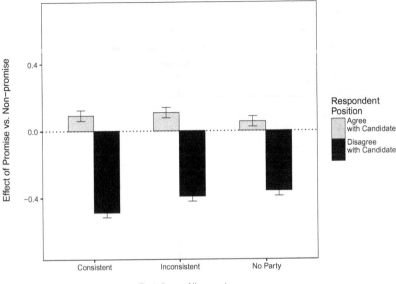

FIGURE 6.2 Effect of promising along party lines

Note: This figure reports the effect of promises on candidate preference, the β value of the OLS regression of candidate choice and the binary variable promise. The effects have been moderated both by whether the candidate's statement aligns with the typical gun control stance of the candidate's party, and by whether the respondent agrees with the candidate or not. The bar denotes the 95% confidence interval of the estimates.

who disagreed with the promise viewed co-partisans and other-party candidates with equal disdain. At the same time, assigning a party has a small effect on treatment differences. The general pattern holds of promises benefiting like-minded candidates and hurting candidates if voters disagree with the promise.

The other way to think about how party might matter is with respect to how positions align with issues. Figure 6.2 shows the differences between candidates who make promises on gun control in accordance with their party's dominant position and those who contradict the party line. Overall, whether candidates are aligned with the party line has no positive effect. Rather, there is a slight, but significant, disadvantage for candidates who promise along partisan lines among voters who disagree with the stance. Voters are slightly less repulsed by candidates who act against partisan lines in taking a position the voter finds disagreeable than candidates who do so toeing the line. While research suggests that candidates who make promises that defy party dogma are more likely to keep them – which should make those candidates more distasteful to voters who do not want to them to keep a particular promise – this finding does not align with expectations of future candidate follow-through, which does not reflect an effect of alignment with the party line. Rather, it corresponds to a slight decrease in negative ratings of candidates who make promises outside of party lines, perhaps indicating a mild preference for candidates seen as "mavericks" (Ditto and Mastronarde, 2009).

These data reveal three insights about the impact of promises. First, partisan information reveals a very similar pattern to the results from Chapter 5 where partisan information was not considered. However, the results here reveal larger differences than when partisan effects are not explicitly controlled for. Even when the candidate's party is different from the respondent's or when the candidate's position is inconsistent with the typical party position, the polarizing effect of promises is larger than when no party information is mentioned. Second, respondents prefer co-partisans they agree with and candidates they agree with whose party is not specified to out-partisans they agree with or candidates with no specified party who they agree with. This may indicate that the uncertainty from lack of partisan information may have translated into a lack of support for candidates generally, even when the ideological position was consistent. But party has quite different effects for candidates respondents disagree with. They have greater objection to candidates they disagree with if the party is specified than if it is not specified, but the party affiliation itself has no impact on their degree of dislike. This reaffirms not only that the polarizing effect of promises is sustained in the presence of partisan information but also that the effect is larger when party information is controlled for. Finally, the changes in candidate preferences when partisan information is revealed do not correspond to differences in perceived future action. Rather, they correspond to a slight decrease in the negative effect of promising on candidate traits. This suggests that candidates are perceived as slightly more honest when they promise against party lines. As this could potentially suggest lowered expectations for pandering (promising against party lines would definitely be more costly and a stronger signal of commitment), this may have important implications for candidates.

Overall, this experiment confirms the robustness of the promise study with respect to partisan information. Adding the partisan information increased the overall effects found previously and continues to confirm the theory that promises polarize voters. That voters may pick up partisan information from whether candidates promise or not is an interesting suggestion for future attention, especially given the literature on issue ownership.

6.2 STUDY 2: PROMISES AND OVERSATURATION

The previous experiment allowed me to test how statements affect vote choice in the presence of partisan cues that exist in most elections. I now turn to the impact when candidates take stances on multiple issues. Here, I use a second experiment to further examine the mediation pathway to better answer how promises affect expectations of follow-through as well as changes in the status quo. The Oversaturation Experiment tests the connection between promises and candidate commitment. It also allows me to measure if promises alter expectations for policy change as well as changing expectations for what individual candidates will do when elected.

6.2.1 Design

For this experiment, I make an important and realistic assumption about candidate commitment: Candidates have a fixed amount of time and influence in the policy realm. This should mean that if a candidate makes more commitments on a larger number of issues, the chances of the candidate following through on any one of those issues decreases. As a result, I manipulate the candidate's position on gun control, and the number of promises that a candidate makes, essentially creating a 2 × 2 experiment.

First, I presented respondents with a candidate and tell them how many promises the candidate has made over the course of the campaign. The treatment described a group investigating campaign websites by saying, "A nonpartisan group analyzes political candidates' websites for the upcoming election." Then the statement introduced the respondents to a candidate and how many promises are on a candidate's website, randomly drawn from 1, 3, 5, 9, 12, and 18 promises, so that there was either a single promise or multiple promises (see Figure 6.4 for an example).

I then gave the respondents one of the candidate's promises on gun control and asked them how they expect the candidate to act on the issue of gun control and how respondents expected the status quo to change (or not) if the candidate was elected. The respondents were told that the candidate made a promise on gun control. The position was then randomized so that the candidate said, "I promise that I [will/will not] work to make gun control stricter" (see Figure 6.3). The respondents were then asked what they think the candidate would be most likely to do if

YouGov

A nonpartisan group analyzes political candidates' websites for the upcoming election. On one candidate's website, the group found **3 promises on various issues**.

One of the candidate's promises was: "I promise that I **will** work to make gun control stricter."

If the candidate is elected, do you think the candidate will...

○ Work to make gun control laws <u>stricter</u>

○ Do <u>nothing</u> on gun control laws

○ Work to make gun control laws <u>less strict</u>

>

FIGURE 6.3 Example of candidate action question

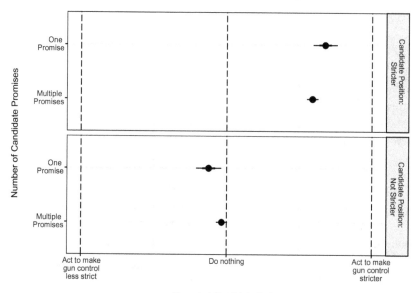

Expected Candidate Action

FIGURE 6.4 Expected candidate action

Note: This figure shows the mean expected action for candidates who have made one promise on the issue of gun control, and for candidates who have made three or more promises on gun control. The broader band indicates the standard error and the wider band is the 95% confidence interval around the mean.

elected: increase gun control, do nothing on gun control, or decrease gun control. Finally, I asked the respondents what they think will happen to gun control policy in the candidate's district if the candidate was elected: laws would become stricter, not change, or become less strict.

While I could consider each level of promise a separate treatment, I first combine the multiple promises into one group, and the single promise into another. I anticipated that candidates who make one promise will be perceived as more likely to follow through and realize a policy shift than candidates who make multiple promises. And, while the group sizes are relatively small to differentiate between all levels of promises, I anticipate a general negative trend in expecting the candidate to act or realize policy associated with each increased number of promises.

6.2.2 Results

The experiment ran in an omnibus survey conducted by YouGov in May 2014 and was fielded to 2,000 respondents.[1] For this analysis, I look first at the difference in means between candidates who make only one promise and candidates who make multiple promises. I then break down the analysis by the number of promises made by the candidate, and the expected candidate action and policy in the candidate's district.

Figure 6.4 shows the mean expected action of the candidate by the candidate's position and whether the candidate promised on no other issues or at least one other issue. For candidates promising stricter gun control, making promises on other issues slightly attenuates the perceived likelihood that the candidate will make gun control stricter ($\mu_{difference} = 0.09$, $p < 0.03$). For candidates promising not to make gun control stricter, the mean is relatively close to the neutral position, where more respondents believed that the candidate would not make gun control stricter. Respondents believed that candidates only promising not to make gun control stricter were more likely to move policy toward making gun control less strict than were candidates who promised on multiple issues ($\mu_{difference} = 0.09$, $p < 0.03$). While technically this is not what the candidate is promising, a greater number of respondents believe that a single promise on the issue makes a candidate more likely to act to decrease gun control.

The questions on policy change continue to support the idea that promises do indicate higher levels of action (see Figure 6.5). First, candidates promising to increase gun control are seen as more likely to do so if they make only one promise on gun control ($\mu_{difference} = 0.10$, $p < 0.02$). Overall, however, respondents are somewhat skeptical of a candidate's ability to move policy on gun control. Just under half of

---

[1] This experiment followed the experiment in Chapter 7. Because I have similar results from Mechanical Turk that are displayed in the Appendix to this chapter, I am not concerned about spillover from one experiment to the other.

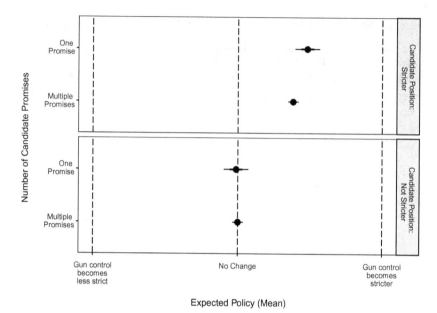

FIGURE 6.5 Expected gun control policy

Note: This figure shows the mean expected policy for candidates who have made one promise on the issue of gun control, and for candidates who have made three or more promises on gun control. The broader band indicates the standard error and the wider band is the 95% confidence interval around the mean.

the respondents believe that a candidate promising to work to make gun control stricter will actually be able to do so. Conversely, regardless of the number of promises that candidates make on gun control, respondents perceive candidates as unlikely to change policy on the issue ($\mu_{difference} = 0.01, p < 0.40$). Perhaps it is the attenuation between action and policy that makes voters skeptical of promise-keeping, and potentially dishonest.

Looking at this data by the number of promises underlines respondents' lack of expectation of change on the issue, but it also indicates that increasing the number of promises does decrease the value of the promise. Figure 6.6 shows the curve of expected candidate action by the number of promises the candidate makes. Expectation for action decreases as the number of promises increases for candidates promising on stricter gun control. For the candidate promising not to make gun control stricter, there is the opposite upward trend, so that the candidate who promises on one issue is seen as more likely to act to decrease gun control than the

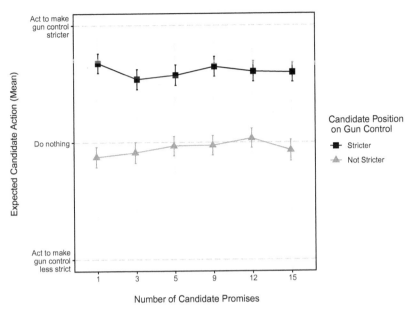

FIGURE 6.6 Expected candidate action by number of promises: YouGov

Note: This figure shows the mean expected action for the candidate's district by the number of promises they have made. The band around the mean is the 95% confidence interval.

candidate who promises on other issues. After three promises, the trend lines for both curves flatten out, and there is very little difference seen between candidates who promise on five different issues and candidates who promise on eighteen different issues.

As expected, then, respondents believe candidates who make one promise are seen as more likely to follow through on that issue than candidates who make multiple promises, and the impact of an additional promise levels out after three promises. At the same time, respondents' expectation of follow-through never completely disappears based on the number of promises. Thus, there is a slight oversaturation effect for promising, but the additional promises do not change whether or not the respondents think the candidate will follow through in general.

Looking at the expectations for gun control policy in the candidate's district shows somewhat similar trends, but insignificant differences between the promise numbers and outcomes. The results are shown in Figure 6.7. Based on the means analysis above, it is not surprising that

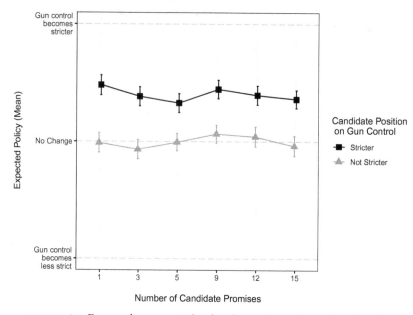

FIGURE 6.7 Expected gun control policy by number of promises: YouGov

Note: This figure shows the mean expected policy for the candidate's district by the number of promises they have made. The band around the mean is the 95% confidence interval.

the trends seen in the previous graphs are not found here. Indeed, there is almost zero difference between expectations for how policy will change if the candidate is elected. The main impact of promises, then, seems more to increase the likelihood that a candidate will follow through rather than that the candidate will be successful in implementing the policy that is promised. (Note that I repeated this entire experiment on Amazon's Mechanical Turk. The general findings remain the same for both studies, though the curves for the Mechanical Turk sample are smoother than the YouGov sample. These results are in the Appendix to this chapter.)

The results from this experiment also indicate that while respondents have an increased expectation that candidates will follow through on the issue of gun control if they make a promise on the issue, their expectations for policy if the candidate is elected do not reflect as much confidence. The results for the stricter candidates are notably less than expectations for action, though the results for the not-stricter candidate remain about the same. Most respondents see candidates as being unlikely to have an impact on gun control policy, which indicates that promising is not necessarily seen as altering policy expectations as much as it changes expectations of follow-through.[2]

For each graph, the results are not symmetric for the two positions the candidate may take. In part, this result stems from the fact that the positions themselves are not symmetric. The candidate who promises not to make gun control stricter may be promising simply to take no action, to make gun control less strict, or to block legislation that makes gun control stricter. (The previous experiment also shows asymmetric results. See the Chapter 5 appendix for the breakdown of the promise experiment graphs by candidate position.) I would expect that the results would more closely mirror each other if the candidate clearly stated that he would make gun control less strict.

This experiment answers a few questions about how promises function prospectively. First, it further tests the relationship between candidate promises and perceptions of commitment to act when in office. The responses regarding action indicate that respondents do believe that candidates who make a commitment to an issue are more likely to act on that issue, and in the manner that was promised. Second, this experiment provides further insight into the contrast between candidate intentions and policy outcomes: While voters believe that candidates are more committed to their promised actions and that candidates will follow through on them, they also are skeptical about whether or not the candidate will realize the policy outcome. Finally, this experiment indicates another limitation of promising: Voters recognize commitment in limited form. While they still believe that a candidate will follow through on a promise if the candidate has made promises on other issues, more promises on other issues tend to produce greater skepticism that candidates will follow through on the initial promise *and* that they will realize policy outcomes on that issue.

---

[2] Promising might still increase expectations of policy relative to non-promising levels, but I do not have a comparative non-promising difference. It is also possible that these findings are issue specific, though given the state of gridlock, Congress, and partisan attitudes (Anderson, Butler, and Harbridge-Yong, 2020), other issues may appear no different.

6.3 CONCLUSION

Together, the studies in this chapter add to the evidence that promises matter for voter evaluations of candidates. They broadly test the robustness of both of the promise experiments from Chapter 5 and provide evidence to support the idea that promises polarize voters. They also demonstrate that promises operate as my theory would predict when we consider how voters respond to promises in the presence of party information or promises on other issues.

In particular, the data shows that in the context of a fuller set of information found in typical races, promises matter to voters. This chapter illustrates that there is some benefit to candidates for promising on issues where there might be greater uncertainty, for instance where candidates promise on issues against party lines. As a robustness check for Chapter 5, it also demonstrates that the effects are even stronger than stated there, because some respondents seem to use candidates' promises as cues to determine the candidates' party; when party is stated, regardless of whether the party agrees with that of the candidates, the effect is significantly stronger than we see when no party is listed. The partisan results are particularly important, because while some local elections are nonpartisan, most are partisan.

Second, promises matter in part because they change expectations about actions rather than realized policy. This finding complements the wealth of documentation that voters tend to think elected officials do not follow through on their promises by showing that voters prospectively doubt promise fulfillment. In contrast, however, voters do still think candidates will be more likely to work on their promised position and this helps confirm the explanation I advanced in Chapter 5 of voters' tendency to perceive candidates who make promises to be both more likely to act *and* less honest. This chapter suggests that voters understand candidates' limited ability to follow through on promises and that they also anticipate that candidates will be more inclined to work to fulfill promises when they make fewer.

The data presented in the last three chapters makes the compelling case that promises act as signals of commitment, and as such alter voter evaluations of candidates. The next step in my analysis is to consider whether voters continue to hold candidates who promise to a higher level of commitment after they have been elected. To this end, Chapter 7 discusses how voters view commitment of promises retrospectively, by examining how voters evaluate elected officials and how they have acted on campaign statements while in office.

APPENDIX

6.A Study 2

6.A.1 Study 2 Sample

TABLE 6.2 *YouGov sample: Oversaturation Experiment*

Demographic	Minimum	Maximum	Mean	Std. Error
Age	19.00	93.00	48.97	0.37
Female	0.00	1.00	0.53	0.01
White	0.00	1.00	0.72	0.01
Married	0.00	1.00	0.50	0.01
Party	−3.00	3.00	−0.34	0.05
Ideology	−2.00	2.00	0.09	0.02
Employment	0.00	2.00	0.85	0.02
Education	1.00	6.00	3.37	0.03
Registered voter	0.00	1.00	0.98	0.00
Interest in news	1.00	7.00	1.84	0.03

6.B Study 2 Replication on Mechanical Turk

6.B.1 Study 2: Mechanical Turk Sample

TABLE 6.3 *Mechanical Turk sample: Oversaturation Experiment*

Demographic	Minimum	Maximum	Mean	Std. Error
Female	0.00	1.00	0.38	0.02
White	0.00	1.00	0.77	0.02
Party	−3.00	3.00	−0.76	0.07
Education	1.00	6.00	3.99	0.05
Registered voter	0.00	1.00	0.75	0.25
Interest in news	1.00	4.00	2.09	0.03

6.B.2 Mechanical Turk Results

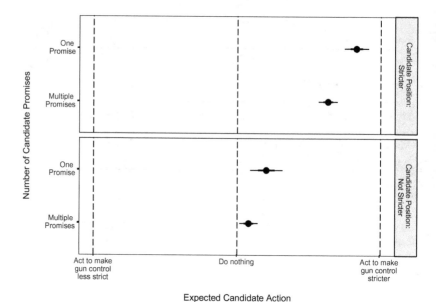

FIGURE 6.8 Expected candidate action: Mechanical Turk

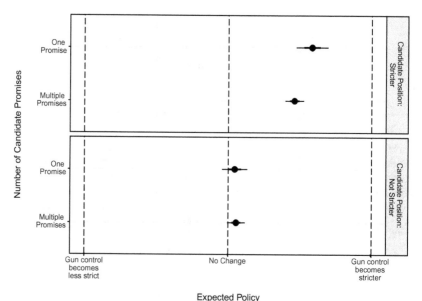

FIGURE 6.9 Expected gun control policy: Mechanical Turk

Note: *These graphs show the mean expected policy for the candidate's district where the candidate has made one promise on the issue of gun control, and for the candidate who has made three or more promises on gun control. A −1 indicates that gun control will become less strict and 1 indicates the candidate will become stricter. The broader band indicates the standard error and the wider band is the 95% confidence interval around the mean.*

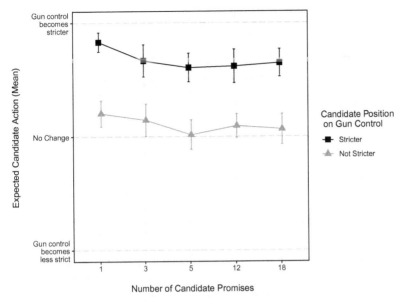

FIGURE 6.10 Expected candidate action by number of promises: Mechanical Turk

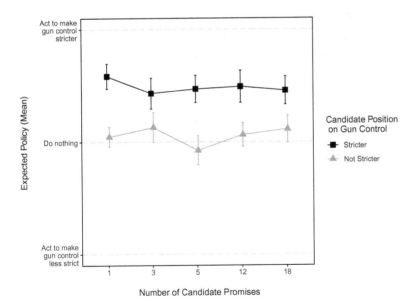

FIGURE 6.11 Expected gun control policy by number of promises: Mechanical Turk

Note: *These graphs show the mean expected action for candidates by the number of promises they have made. A −1 indicates that the candidate will act to decrease gun control and 1 indicates the candidate will act to increase gun control. The band around the mean is the 95% confidence interval.*

7

Promising in Retrospect

Republican opposition to Barack Obama's signature legislation, the Affordable Care Act (ACA), began as soon as it was signed into law, and two days later, Republicans in the House had proposed a bill for repeal. Promises to "repeal and replace" began springing up among Republicans vying for the 2016 presidential nomination, and it was an important feature of many Republican campaigns that election cycle (e.g., GOP, 2016). When Trump won the presidency, the House, and the Senate, many in the GOP claimed they had a "mandate" to overturn healthcare.

Indeed, healthcare became an early priority of the Trump administration, and the Affordable Healthcare Act (AHCA), which would remove key features of the ACA, passed the House. It was a widely unpopular act, garnering just 17 percent approval in a March Quinnipiac Poll (Quinnipiac University Poll, 2017). Immediately after its passage, the Cook Political Report estimated the Republicans would lose twenty seats in the House and that the bill was "consistent with past scenarios that have generated a midterm wave" (Vladimirov, 2017). When anchor George Stephanopoulos asked Ryan about this on ABC's "This Week," Speaker Paul Ryan dismissed it, arguing that the Republicans were addressing an important problem. But "more importantly," he said, he and his colleagues would be "keeping our word" (Ryan, 2017). Ryan continued,

People expect their elected leaders that they run and campaign on doing something, they expect them to do that. And that's what we're doing: we're keeping our word. And, I would argue that we would spell disaster for ourselves politically . . . if we go back on our word. This is us keeping our word.

Ryan's summary emphasizes a basic understanding of promissory representation: It is not just that voters expect candidates to campaign on positions they will actually work to carry out but that candidates know that those expectations are attached to future elections. In essence, promises as signaling mechanisms can only have an effect if candidates who send a false signal bear a cost. This chapter demonstrates that the distinction between promise and non-promise statements matters retrospectively as well as prospectively, in that the cost is higher for breaking a promise. The assertions of the prior chapters suggest that voters will view candidates who promise as more likely to follow through on a promise than candidates who make less firm commitments. Carrying this over to a retrospective setting, voters may be more disappointed in a candidate who does not follow through on a statement on which they appear more committed compared to if they had initially made a less firm commitment. I would also anticipate that voters would more highly reward an elected official who kept a promise than if that official had less firmly committed on an issue with a milder commitment. This chapter investigates these implications from my theory. It focuses on how promises affect voter decision-making when voters know whether the candidate has broken or kept a promise. In particular, I provide an answer to these questions: How do voters perceive candidates who break their promises compared to candidates who made a weaker commitment based on their subsequent behavior? In addition, do voters reward candidates who promise more than they reward candidates with whom they agree?

In Chapter 2, I argued that campaign promises matter because they indicate the candidate's increased commitment to an issue position. Promises should matter because a candidate who has promised is not only repositioning but also breaking their commitment to voters. Thus, voters should have a decrease in approval of elected officials who promised and do not keep their word relative to an elected official who did not promise and do not keep their word. At the same time, there should be an increase in preferences for candidates who promise and keep their word relative to candidates who do not promise and keep their word. (Table 7.1 summarizes these hypotheses in the context of the broader theory. See Table 7.4 in the Appendix for a more comprehensive set of hypotheses that focus on the more intricate features of this experiment.)

I also focus on how keeping and breaking promises matters to voters. In Chapters 5 and 6, I have shown that promises are important

TABLE 7.1 *Hypotheses: Promises affect voter behavior retrospectively*

Hypothesis	Study 1: Paired-Candidate	Study 2 Excuses
Voters recognize promises retrospectively Among elected officials who act in accordance with the positions they have claimed to hold, voters reward promisers more than non-promisers, and among candidates who do not act in accordance with their stated positions, voters punish promisers more than non-promisers.	X	X
Promises change expectations for follow-through and character evaluations Generally, voters will see officials who follow through as more honest and more likely to follow through in the future than candidates who do not. They will also see promisers who follow through as more likely to follow through in the future and more honest than candidates who follow through on weaker commitments. Officials who promise and do not follow through will be seen as less likely to follow through in the future and less honest than candidates who violate weaker commitments.	X	
Promisers will be viewed as less open-minded than non-promisers when they follow through. Promisers will be viewed as more open-minded than non-promisers when they do not follow through.	X	
Broken promises are not ignored Excuses made by promise-breakers will not lead to ratings of future follow-through, honesty, or open-mindedness that are as high as ratings for a candidate who repositions but does not promise.		X

because they alter expectations of candidate follow-through as well as candidate traits. In my theory, I argue that promises should alter how respondents view candidate traits and future action, as they consider future representation by candidates. Compared to candidates who take the same position but do not promise, I hypothesize that candidates who promise and follow through on their initial position will be rated as more likely to follow through on that issue in the future. I expect to find that respondents will view promisers who follow through as more honest than non-promisers, and as less open-minded than non-promisers who take the same position. In addition, I anticipate that promisers who go back on their word will be seen as less honest than non-promisers and, perhaps, more open-minded.

To understand the extent to which promises matter retrospectively and how they impact voter decision-making, I present the results of a survey experiment. In the Retrospective Promise Experiment, I report the respondents with two candidates, one who promises and one who does not, and control for the description of the positions and actions the candidate took in office. I manipulate whether the candidates agree or disagree with the respondent on gun control, and whether the candidates act in accordance with their promise or not. I then ask the respondents which candidate they prefer. Finally, I ask the respondents to rate expectations for future follow-through on the candidate's initial position as well as the candidate's honesty and open-mindedness in office. I show that voters do consider the commitment invoked through promises as they evaluate elected officials. They view promisers more positively for following through on their position, and more negatively than non-promisers for not following through on their position. In an insight potentially useful to future candidates, I also find that, for candidates who take a position in the election with which they did not agree, respondents will still object to violations of promises when the elected officials implement an action the voter prefers. Even when a candidate acts in the way that a voter prefers, if the candidate stated the opposite position during the election, voters still rate candidates who promised higher than those who made a weaker commitment.

Finally, I am also interested in understanding how long-lasting the consequences of breaking a promise are. Promises can only act as signals if the effects of breaking a promise are difficult to overcome. As such, I test how easily candidates can distance themselves from the ill-effects of breaking a promise. I allow the respondents to see one of several excuses found in the presidential debates and ask the respondents (a) how much they expect the candidate to follow through on his initial position in the future; (b) how honest the candidate is; and (c) how open-minded the candidate is. I expect that a promise-breaker will receive slightly better ratings after making an excuse but will be judged more harshly than if he had not broken his promise.

To test how difficult it is for candidates to escape the consequences of a broken promise, I use an extension of the Retrospective Promise Experiment. In the Excuses Experiment, I randomly assign each respondent one of four different excuses made by the promise-breaker to determine if excuses can increase a respondent's opinion of a candidate who broke their promise. In this experiment, I anticipate that some excuses will allow the promise-breaker to improve the respondents' view of them, but that the change in attitude toward the candidate will not be as great as if the candidate had not promised in the first place or as great as if the candidate had not broken their word.

7.1 THE RETROSPECTIVE PROMISE EXPERIMENT

I present an experiment that measures the impact of breaking or keeping a promise. The experiment contains three steps. I first measure the respondent's position on gun control. Second, I present the respondent with two candidates who have taken a position on gun control and voted in accordance or against that position. Third, I ask the respondent to rate candidates' follow-through on their initial position, honesty, and open-mindedness. This survey experiment measures respondents' preference for candidates who state a position or who make a promise when the voter sees the candidate's action.

7.1.1 Measurement

This survey experiment has three parts, and it is quite similar to the experiment presented in Chapter 5. I measure respondent positions on gun control prior to presenting the experimental content using the same two-response formulation of the question: "Do you favor or oppose gun control?" I give the respondent the options, "Favor" and "Oppose."

Next, I present a paired-candidate treatment quite similar to the Paired-Candidate Experiment in Chapter 5. I describe two features of the candidates: a statement on gun control made during their campaign, and a vote on gun control made while they were in office. I manipulated the respondent–candidate agreement and whether the candidates act in accordance with or in opposition to their stated position on gun control. I then ask respondents which candidate they prefer.

I present the information to the respondents as follows. First, I ask the respondents to consider politicians who have taken positions on gun control and are running for reelection. I then present Candidate A with two bullet points. The first point describes how Candidate A discussed gun control while campaigning. It says, "Before the election, he [promised/did not promise] [to/not to] increase gun control."[1] The second bullet point describes how Candidate A voted on a bill about gun control. It reads "After the election, he voted [to/not to] increase gun control." Together, these clearly indicate if Candidate A keeps his word on gun control or not. I then present Candidate B with two bullet points with similar information. The candidates' position on gun control is randomly selected between the position "to increase gun control" or "not to increase gun control." The candidate can either vote "to increase gun control" or vote "not to increase gun control." Both candidates maintain the same position on gun control and both act in a way that is consistent or inconsistent with their previously stated position. This allows me to measure respondent preference for a candidate who promises and keeps his word against a candidate who does not promise and keeps his word. The content of the candidate profiles can be found in Table 7.2.[2] (See Figure 7.1 for an example.)

Thus, the information respondents see depicts Candidate A and Candidate B having the same position, and the same action (i.e., either in accordance with or in opposition to their stated positions), but one has made a promise and one has not. The position the candidates take on gun control is randomized independently of whether or not the candidate acts in accordance with their stated position. While this format does not allow respondents to differentiate promises from non-promises themselves, I find similar results when I use the same language as in the previous experiment. Additionally, at this point I have also demonstrated

---

[1] The candidate is described with male gender pronouns simply to control for any inferences made about gender between the two candidates.

[2] In all other studies in this book, I have included statements that the candidates make instead of simply indicating that the candidates have promised or not. Here, I do not include the full statements for three reasons. First, the complete statements largely yielded the same trends in pretesting as summaries do here. Second, I have demonstrated in Chapter 4 that voter definitions of promises match those proposed in this book, and since I have already submitted evidence of the connection between promises and increased commitment and expectations for action, I do not feel that this experiment needs to directly test the content of the statements. Finally, asking respondents to read and consider full statements is a time-intensive task, and simply indicating whether the statement is a promise or not greatly reduced the labor and time required for the task. I am not concerned that the formulation here is what is driving the results presented.

TABLE 7.2 *Content of candidate profiles*

Position	Increase Gun Control	Not Increase Gun Control
Statement (Before the election...)	...he promised to increase gun control.	...he promised not to increase gun control.
	...he said, but did not promise, to increase gun control.	...he said, but did not promise, not to increase gun control.
Action (After the election...)	he voted to increase gun control.	he voted not to increase gun control.

Note: This table shows the full text found in the candidate profiles. The full profile is selected as follows. One of the two positions is selected for the candidate pair. The candidates are then assigned the statements within the pair (though the order is randomized). Then, one of the candidate actions is independently and randomly selected to use in both candidate profiles.

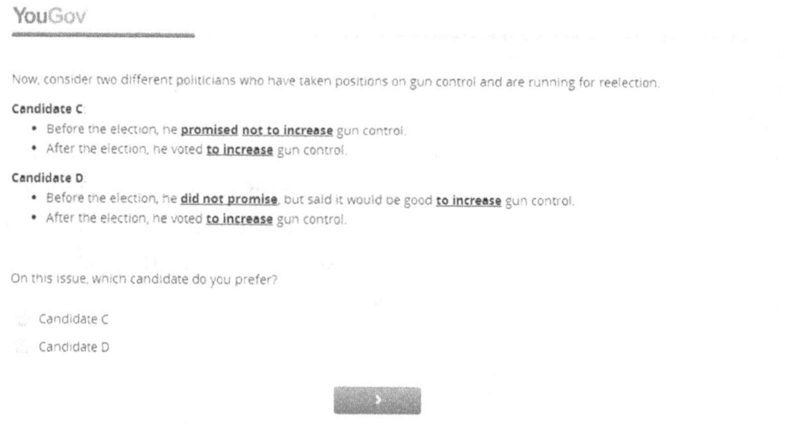

YouGov

Now, consider two different politicians who have taken positions on gun control and are running for reelection.

Candidate C
- Before the election, he **promised not to increase** gun control.
- After the election, he voted **to increase** gun control.

Candidate D
- Before the election, he **did not promise**, but said it would be good **to increase** gun control.
- After the election, he voted **to increase** gun control.

On this issue, which candidate do you prefer?

◯ Candidate C

◯ Candidate D

[›]

FIGURE 7.1 Experiment example

that respondents do differentiate between promises and non-promises – both in perceptions of commitment and classifications of what constitutes a promise.

There is another distinction between the prospective paired-candidate experiment and the retrospective experiment. Heretofore, my experiments have left the candidate's office ambiguous. The candidates could have been in any level of legislative or executive branches, and no previous public record is specified beyond the length of time the candidate is in office. Here, the candidates must have been serving in a legislative position since they are voting on a bill. This change was made to more clearly indicate that the candidate has kept or broken a promise without having to directly use that language. Acting consistently or inconsistently with a stated position is clearer and simpler to indicate with a voting record than with other means of action that executive officials have at their disposal. Also, note that the office the candidates are running for is not given; it could be a legislative position or an executive position.[3]

In the YouGov sample, the survey ended at this point. However, on Mechanical Turk, the survey continued by asking the respondents to assess each candidate's likelihood to follow through on their initial action as well as the candidate's honesty and open-mindedness. In order to remind the respondents of the candidate information, I separately repeat each candidate's information for the respondent, presented in exactly the same manner as before. I then ask the respondent, "How well do the following statements describe Candidate [A/B/C/D]?"

I then present the respondents with a grid where the left column contains the statement the respondent is asked about, and the right column contains a sliding scale from 1 to 7. The scale ends are labeled "Not at all" and "Extremely well." The first phrase asks, "Likely [to/not to] increase gun control in future," where the direction the respondent is asked about corresponds to the initial position that the candidate took. The second

---

[3] It is possible that explicitly making the candidate make a promise in a legislative environment yields different results than if the candidate held an executive office. And, these results might seem to build a separate line of inquiry than those presented in Chapter 3. However, it is unlikely the results will be much different than if I had indicated more vaguely whether the candidates worked for stricter gun control. In both scenarios, candidates would keep or break their promises; what would differ is the metric of whether or not the candidates kept or broke their promises. While the determination of what constitutes a kept promise or an action consistent with a position might differ for an executive or a legislative figure, the ultimate attitude about if the promise is kept or not should not change. Since I am simply measuring the impact of a kept or broken promise on judgments of candidates, it makes sense to have an unambiguous way to indicate that a candidate has acted consistently or inconsistently with a previously stated position. Perhaps in later work it would be useful to measure how a voter determines whether or not a candidate keeps or breaks his promise; but that is a separate line of inquiry that is beyond the scope of the questions at hand. In addition, using candidates with a legislative background is not necessarily a departure from the previous chapters. In Chapter 3, I described how many of the candidates running for president come from legislative positions and have to explain voting histories. In so doing, candidates refer to their own voting record and that of their opponent. Furthermore, candidates do not simply discuss voting record in general. They often discuss a candidate's record on specific votes instead. Finally, although some candidates do come from executive posts, many come from legislative posts.

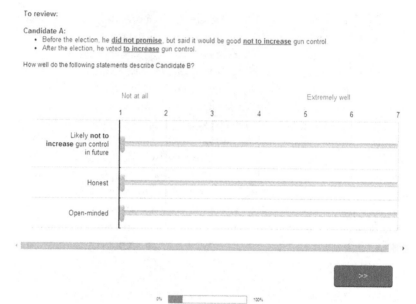

To review:

Candidate A:
- Before the election, he **did not promise**, but said it would be good **not to increase** gun control
- After the election, he voted **to increase** gun control.

How well do the following statements describe Candidate B?

FIGURE 7.2 Measuring the follow-through and traits

phrase says "Honest," and the third phrase reads "Open-minded."[4] After the screen with Candidate A, the respondent sees a similar screen for a different candidate. This time, the chart contains the information for Candidate B, and asks how well the following statements describe Candidate B. An example of how these questions appear is found in Figure 7.2.

To increase the sample size, each respondent receives two candidate pairings, one after the other. The candidates are called, in order of appearance, A, B, C, and D.[5] Each candidate pair that a respondent sees is unique. I use two choice rules to determine how the second set of candidates is determined. In a shorter version of the survey, which includes only the measurement of the main effect, the second pair is chosen to either (a) take different initial positions on gun control, (b) act oppositely from the first pair, or (c) both take different initial positions on gun control and act oppositely from the first pair. That is, if the first pair follows through, then the second pair either follows through but takes the opposite position or repositions and takes the same position. In Mechanical Turk, where I measure the main effects, future action, and character, if the first pairing

---

[4] These questions were only asked on the Mechanical Turk version of the survey.
[5] The results do not change if I only look at the respondents' first candidate pair.

repositions, the second follows through. The position the candidate takes is randomly decided for each pair.

Because I am attaching candidate actions to promises and subject agreement, this experiment produces four treatment groups: candidates who follow through with whom respondents agree, candidates who follow through with whom respondents disagree, candidates who do not follow through where respondents agree with the original position and not the action, and candidates who do not follow through where respondents agree with the action but not the initial position. Based on these treatments, I have two expectations. First, I expect to find that the mean preference for a promising candidate is greater than the mean preference for a non-promiser if the candidate follows through on his initial position. My theory predicts the opposite is true for a candidate who does not follow through on who repositions. Second, I expect to see that respondents who disagree with a candidate will rate that candidate more harshly than respondents who agree with the candidate.

As with the prospective pathway, I anticipated that agreement will have a minimal effect on how respondents perceive candidate follow through and candidate character measures. I anticipated that voters will expect candidates who promise and follow through to follow through in the future at a higher rate than candidates who followed through on a weaker commitment, and the opposite to be true for candidates who break a promise and candidates who failed to follow through on a weaker commitment. Similarly, I anticipated ratings on candidate honesty will reflect the same pattern: Promisers will receive higher ratings when they follow through and lower ratings when they do not follow through. Open-mindedness should work slightly differently from honesty in this situation. Respondents might believe that candidates who break their word are more open-minded and candidates who follow through are less open-minded.

7.1.2 Results: Effects of Keeping and Breaking a Promise

The Retrospective Paired-Candidate Experiment was fielded on two platforms: a nationally representative sample that measured the main dependent variables, and a convenience sample that measured all the variables. Data from the nationally representative sample was collected on an omnibus survey run through the Stanford Laboratory of American Values conducted by YouGov in April 2014. The survey was given to 2,000 adults randomly selected from YouGov's online panel. The selection process was designed so that the sample matches the adult US population with respect to gender, age, race, education, party identification, ideology, and level of political interest based on the 2010 American Community Survey and 2012 Current Population Survey. A description of the respondents can be found in the Appendix to this chapter. The full version of this survey experiment was conducted on Amazon's Mechanical Turk in March 2014. The sample included 298 subjects. A description of the characteristics of this sample appears in the Appendix to this chapter.[6] This version contains the main effects of the survey as well as measurements of expected candidate action on gun control in the future and candidate character.

To determine the difference between voter opinion of candidates who promise versus those who do not promise, I again calculate the effect of making a promise on candidate choice.[7] A positive difference indicates that a candidate would do better to promise, while a negative difference indicates that a candidate would do better not to promise.

Figure 7.3 displays the results for this experiment, moderated by candidate and respondent position, as well as whether the candidate followed through on the initial position or not. The left side of the figure displays the results for candidates who do not follow through. For all groups, respondents strongly preferred the candidate who did not initially promise on gun control ($\mu_p = 0.08$, $\mu_{np} = 0.92$, $p < 0.001$). Where the candidate favors gun control, there is a small and significant decrease in the effect of promising among respondents who oppose stricter gun control. Overall, however, candidate position has less of an effect if candidates fail to follow through on their promises.

The results when a candidate follows through are on the right side of the figure. For all treatment groups, there is a positive and significant effect of promising ($\mu_p = 0.68$, $\mu_{np} = 0.32$, $p < 0.001$). Respondents who disagree with the candidate's position approve of the promiser significantly less often than respondents who agree with the candidate's position. It seems that candidates punish and reward the commitment of promisers first rather than considering how the candidate acted on gun control. The result is also largely consistent with previous findings on candidate waffling: candidates do not attract voters by repositioning, even if voters

---

[6] See Chapter 4 for a description of the usefulness and viability of using Amazon's Mechanical Turk to recruit subject pools.

[7] For further information on my approach, see the appendix to Chapter 5.

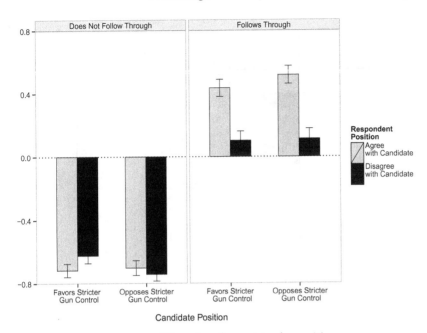

FIGURE 7.3 Effect size of promising by position

Note: This figure shows the effect of promising, calculated as the β value of the OLS regression of candidate choice *and the binary variable* promise. *The results are moderated by candidate and respondent position.*

prefer the candidate's action (Allgeier et al., 1979; Carlson and Dolan, 1985). The results are asymmetric between the gains from promising and following through and the loss of support for promising and breaking that promise. Candidates stand to lose more from breaking a promise, regardless of voter agreement, than they might hope to gain from following through on a promise.

These results largely confirm what I expect from theory. Namely, the promising candidate receiving an almost universal penalty for breaking his promise; the candidate who does not commit to action is preferred to the candidate who commits to action. The candidate who follows through on his promise is significantly preferred over the candidate who merely follows through on his position. Unlike in Chapter 6, whether the respondent agrees or disagrees with the candidate does moderate the respondent's preference for or against a candidate, except in preference for candidates who follow through on a position with which the respondent disagrees.

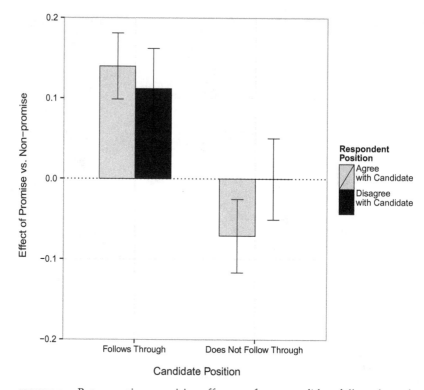

FIGURE 7.4 Retrospective promising effects on future candidate follow-through

Note: These results show the β value of the OLS regression of candidate follow through and the binary variable promise *moderated by the treatment conditions of candidate action and candidate–respondent agreement. The error bar on each bar indicates the 95% confidence interval. For all groups, N = 298.*

Voter perceptions of follow-through, honesty, and open-mindedness were measured on a 7-point scale. For the following results, I have transformed the scale to a 0–1 scale, so that differences represent a percent difference in ratings between candidates who promised and those who did not promise. I also ignore the candidate's position on gun control as it has little effect in this experiment and it makes the treatment groups easier to consider.

Figure 7.4 shows how much respondents expect candidates to follow-through on their initial position in the future. The candidates who followed through are rated higher when candidates promised than when they did not ($\beta_{agree} = 0.14$, $p < 0.001$; $\beta_{disagree} = 0.11$, $p < 0.05$). When respondents agreed with the candidates, they were seen as much more likely to follow through in the future than when the respondents

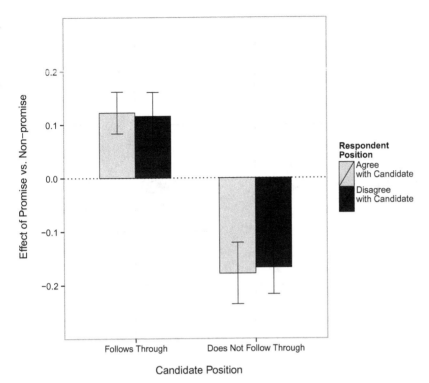

FIGURE 7.5 Retrospective promising effects on candidate honesty

Note: These results show the mean opinion of candidate honesty moderated by the treatment conditions of candidate action and candidate–respondent agreement. The error bar on each bar indicates the 95% confidence interval.

disagreed with the candidates. For candidates who repositioned and promised, respondents who agreed with candidates were uncertain if candidates would follow through in the future ($\beta_{agree} = 0.00$, $p = 1$). Respondents who initially disagreed with the candidates who repositioned differentiated between promisers and non-promisers in their expectations of future follow-through and thought candidates were unlikely to follow through in the future ($\beta_{agree} = 0-0.07$, $p = 0.003$). Candidates in this treatment group act in accordance with the respondent's preferred policy position, and that may alter expectations of follow-through and increase uncertainty around judgments of the candidates.

Figure 7.5 presents the results on candidate honesty. Here, we see that candidates who follow through on their initial position can all be described as honest, while candidates who reposition cannot be described

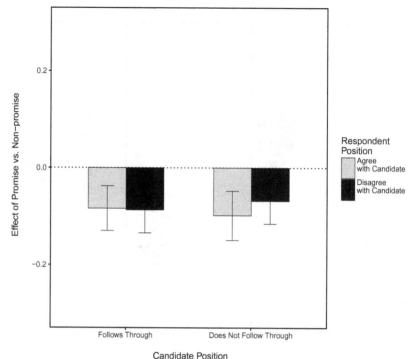

FIGURE 7.6 Retrospective promising effects on candidate open-mindedness

Note: These results show the β value of the OLS regression of candidate open-mindedness *and the binary variable* promise *moderated by the treatment conditions of candidate action and candidate–respondent agreement. The error bar on each bar indicates the 95% confidence interval.*

as honest. In addition, candidates who promised and kept their word were seen as significantly more honest than candidates who do not promise and follow through ($\beta_{agree} = 0.12, p < 0.001$; $\beta_{disagree} = 0.12, p < 0.001$). In contrast, candidates who break their promises are seen as significantly less honest than candidates who did not make a promise but took a position on which they did not follow through ($\beta_{agree} = -0.18, p < 0.001$; $\beta_{disagree} = -0.17, p < 0.001$). Candidates who reposition but did not promise are seen as less honest than candidates who follow through on their initial position, but more honest than candidates who promise and break their promise.

Finally, judgments about candidate open-mindedness were somewhat different from honesty but more similar to what would be expected from Chapter 5. Figure 7.6 shows these results. In all conditions, the effect of promising is negative, meaning that non-promisers are seen as more open-minded than promisers. It might seem natural that a candidate who changes his stance would be considered more open-minded, but the data instead shows that the mean rating for open-mindedness is larger among both promisers and non-promisers ($\mu_{ft} = 0.58$, $\mu_{nft} = 0.52$, $p < 0.001$). This seems to underline that respondents are signaling approval for commitments and behavior rather than approval for outcomes in answering the questions about candidate traits.

This experiment supports several important hypotheses of my theory, including that perceptions of commitment to positions carry over into retrospective judgments of candidates. In particular, candidates who promise are preferred and perceived as more likely to continue following through, more honest, and more open-minded than candidates who took a similar position but did not promise. This study also seems to underscore the importance of the candidates adhering to actions that mirror campaign statements. Respondents seemed to be more concerned with candidates acting according to their actions than they were concerned about how the actions aligned with their own views of gun control, suggesting that the expectation of candidate follow-through may be even more important than outcome.

7.1.3 Strategic Implications When Voters Consider the Future

Because candidates are likely to calculate whether to make promises based on the future outcomes, there is another opportunity for understanding how promises might be strategically deployed. A candidate may be more inclined to make a promise if they can expect a large gain in the future from following through on their promise. Unlike the prospective case, the retrospective gains from promising are uniform if the promise is kept, even if respondents disagree with the candidates. And, the losses from promising depend on whether or not candidates are able to keep their word. In this sense, there would be no sample population where a candidate could promise, break their word, and gain even when not promising. Instead, I consider how a candidate can gain in the long term based on expectations of their ability to follow through on the promise.

Candidates are not simply considering their ability to gain votes in the current election; they also need to consider the impact of their ability to keep the promise on their future prospects. While there is evidence that candidates attempt to keep their word in office, they cannot be sure they

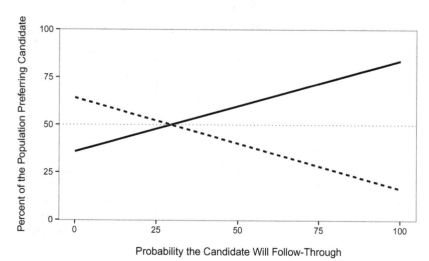

FIGURE 7.7 Projected voter preferences based on probability of not following through for candidates who favor gun Control

Note: This graph presents the projected level of support candidates would find in a district based on whether or not they promised. The solid line represents the candidate who promises; the dashed line presents a candidate who does not.

will be able to do so (Fishel, 1985). Thus, I consider the full range of probabilities that arise with respect to whether candidates will follow through on their word, p, in addition to gains from promising among those they agree with and disagree with. The difference between promising can be calculated as follows:

$$E_r = p(nV(C_KP) + (1 - n)V(C_KN)) + (1 - p)(nV(C_BP) + (1 - n)V(C_BN)).$$

I calculate the expected value of promising for each probability of following through and change in support for gun control. The results of this calculation yield a comparison of the gains and the losses between a candidate promising and making a weaker commitment on each side of the issue. Figures 7.7 and 7.8 display the results graphically for the expected percentage of the vote the candidate should expect to receive. Overall, for candidates who believe in restriction, when they have a 32 percent chance of keeping their word, they should promise on the issue of gun control. Candidates who oppose gun control need about a 33 percent chance of following through on their word to benefit from promising. This indicates that candidates who are dependent on long-term affects of

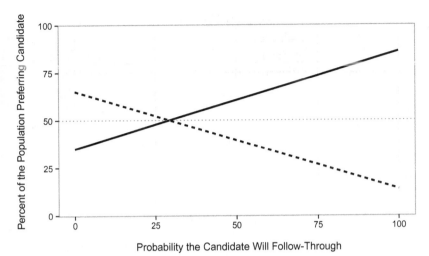

FIGURE 7.8 Projected voter preferences based on probability of not following through for candidates who oppose gun control

Note: This graph presents the projected level of support candidates would find in a district if they promised or not. The solid line represents the candidate who promises; the dashed line presents a candidate who does not.

promising, regardless of their stance on the issue, need to be relatively confident they can fulfill their promise.

7.2 STUDY 2: EXCUSES, EXCUSES

This study tests the robustness of the previous findings by determining how resistant the effects of broken promises are to various types of excuses that candidates can make. Candidates actively try to keep promises, and both external pressure from voters and internal pressure because they promise on issues they care about personally act in concert (Sulkin, 2009). But it is inevitable for some candidates to break campaign promises, and candidates may give reasons, compelling or otherwise, for such failures. For example, Obama promised to close the Guantanamo Bay prison during a stump speech during his 2008 campaign (Baker, 2008). While he issued executive orders and decreased the overall size of the prison population throughout both terms of his presidency, Obama never fulfilled his promise to close Guantanamo Bay (Collins, 2016). Reflecting on how he could have realized this promise (and expressing regret for not), Obama very clearly blamed part of the problem on a lack of consensus between the parties (Jaffe, 2015). While obviously this issue did not prevent Obama's reelection bid, he was heavily criticized for not keeping his word. But this raises the question as to whether candidates can explain away a departure from a promise.

To measure whether or not candidate excuses can sway voters, I examine the influence excuses have on respondents' perceptions of the candidate's likelihood to follow through on his word, honesty, and open-mindedness. I use an addition to the previous experiment to determine if respondents change their minds if candidates can explain why they did not follow through.

7.2.1 Measuring the Success of Excuses

The Excuses Experiment followed the Retrospective Promise Experiment, and builds on those results. After presenting the full version of the Retrospective Promise Experiment, I remind the respondent of the candidate who broke his word by saying, "Recall Candidate A. Candidate A broke his promise [to/not to] increase gun control. He explains his action, saying...."[8] The excuse was randomly chosen from those displayed in Table 7.3. I then ask the respondent how well each of the following statements describes the candidate, and remeasure respondent assessments of the candidate's future follow-through, honesty, and open-mindedness as I did previously. See Figure 7.9 for an example.

The excuse categories I use are similar to excuses made, and the language is changed to fit the issue and generalized to the scenario. For example, the first type of excuse, "Admit Mistake," is similar to George H. W. Bush's statement, explaining his broken promise not to raise taxes. "They get on me, Bill's gotten on me about 'Read my lips.' When I make a mistake, I'll admit it" (Bush, 1992). This excuse simply admits having made a mistake, and urges voters to think about them more holistically rather than judging them on this single instance.

The next excuse, "One of the Crowd," is similar to Hillary Clinton's comment that most policy-makers agreed on the Iraq War vote in 2002: "The consensus was the same, from the Clinton administration to the Bush administration. It was the same intelligence belief that our allies and friends around the world shared" (Clinton, 2004). John Kerry uses

---

[8] Each respondent saw one candidate who failed to follow through on his word in the Mechanical Turk survey.

TABLE 7.3 *List of candidate excuses*

Excuse Type	Phrase
Admit mistake	I made a mistake voting [to/not to] increase gun control. Except for this vote, my record is consistent and shows that I generally vote [not to/to] increase gun control.
One of the crowd	I did vote [to/ not to] increase gun control; but everyone else voted the same way.
More important issues	At the time, we were facing a budget crisis, so voting [to/not to] increase gun control was not a priority.
Partisan	I could not have voted [to/not to] increase gun control; the other party designed the bill and it had flaws.

Note: This table contains excuses for repositioning similar to those found in the presidential election debates. One excuse is presented to respondents explaining why the promiser broke his promise, in order to measure changes in the mediators.

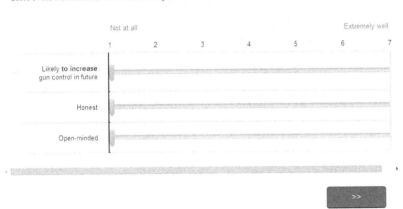

Please think about Candidate B again. Candidate B broke his promise to increase gun control.

He has explained his action, saying: "At the time, we were facing a budget crisis, so voting not to increase gun control was not a priority."

Based on this information, how well do the following statements describe Candidate B?

FIGURE 7.9 Experiment example

a similar defense for his vote on the Patriot Act when he said, "Now, I voted for the Patriot Act. Ninety-nine United States Senators voted for it" (Kerry, 2004). This excuse reflects the idea that even though the candidate is under criticism for a past action, at the time, the candidate felt they were acting as most others would act, and as their constituents wanted them to act.

The third excuse, "More Important Issues," is an excuse that indicates the candidate either did not or could not follow through on a position because there were more important matters to attend to. This type of excuse can indicate that the candidate has been unable to fulfill (or has broken) a promise because of a more pressing, and potentially unexpected, issue. For instance, 9/11 and the Iraq War presented George W. Bush with an unexpected set of issues that altered the course of his presidency. During one of the debates with John Kerry, a voter challenged Bush on his no-spending promises in the previous election and his inaction to prevent more government spending. He explained:

> We're at war. And I'm going to spend what it takes to win the war, more than just 120 billion for Iraq and Afghanistan. We've got to pay our troops more. We have. We've increased money for ammunition and weapons and pay and homeland security. I just told this lady over here we spent–went from 10 to 30 billion dollars to protect the homeland. I think we have an obligation to spend that kind of money.
>
> And you're right, I haven't vetoed any spending bills because we worked together. Non-homeland, non-defense, discretionary spending was rising at 15 percent a year when I got into office. And today, it's less than one percent, because we're working together to try to bring this deficit under control. Like you, I'm concerned about the deficit. But I am not going to shortchange our troops in harm's way. (Bush, 2004)

The final type of excuse I test is the "Partisan" excuse. This excuse suggests it is the other party's fault the bill did not pass or was crafted in such a way that the candidate could not vote for it. This excuse mimics one of the most-cited reason preventing candidates from realizing a campaign promise (Fishel, 1985). For example, Obama blamed his unfulfilled promise on taxes to the Republican party:

> So four years ago I stood on a stage just like this one. Actually it was a town hall, and I said I would cut taxes for middle-class families, and that's what I've done, by $3,600.00. I said I would cut taxes for small businesses, who are the drivers and engines of growth. And we've cut them 18 times. And I want to continue those tax cuts for middle-class families, and for small business.... I'm ready to sign that bill right now. The only reason it's not happening is because Governor Romney's allies in Congress have held the 98 percent hostage because they want tax breaks for the top 2 percent. (Obama, 2012)

In practice, the excuses are much more nuanced and detailed in explanation than I can address in the experiment. Nonetheless, the excuses I use in the experiment capture the main ideas represented in each example. And, the different types of excuses illustrate how candidates attempt to cover a faulty record and are generally instructive as to how easily they can dismiss the effects of a broken promise.

7.2.2 Results

The Excuses Experiment was embedded in the Mechanical Turk survey described in the previous section and fielded in March 2014. It was presented following the Retrospective Paired-Candidate Experiment. Figure 7.10 presents the shift in mean assessments for expectations on future follow-through and candidate traits after the respondents see an excuse made by a promise-breaker. The y-axis shows the categories of excuses that a candidate might make, while the x-axis shows the mean opinion of candidates. The means are shown with both a standard error band and a 95% confidence interval band. The solid, vertical line is the pre-excuse mean for candidates who broke their promises in office. The dashed, vertical line is the mean for candidates who did not promise but did not follow through on their original position in office, given for comparison. The dotted, vertical line at 4 represents the midpoint of the scale.

This chart shows, first, that most of the excuses do shift respondents' expectations of candidate action a significant amount away from the initial negative rating. No excuse convinces respondents that the candidate will follow through in the future, but admitting a mistake and blaming the other party had roughly equivalent impact, greater than the "More Important Issues" excuse. Both of these excuses increase the candidate's assessments to a higher level than a non-promiser who had repositioned.

The next figure is organized the same way, but it displays opinions of candidate honesty. In Figure 7.11, the solid line represents the pre-excuse, mean perceptions of the promise-breaker's honesty. And the dashed line represents the mean expectation of a non-promiser who repositions. Most excuses lead respondents to perceive candidates as more honest, but the "Out of the Crowd" has the opposite effect. Much as with expectations for candidates' future action, admitting having made a mistake and the "Partisan Excuse" performs the best in increasing perceptions of candidate honesty. However, in no case do assessments of promise-breaker honesty approach the midpoint, where respondents see them as particularly

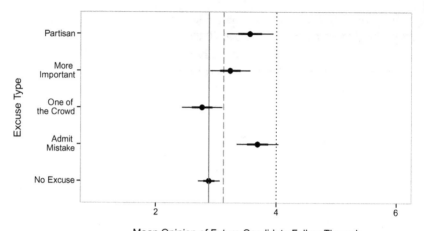

Mean Opinion of Future Candidate Follow-Through

FIGURE 7.10 Effect of excuses on future candidate follow-through

Note: *This figure shows the mean opinion of future candidate follow-through on his initial position after having broken his promise. The longer error bar indicates the 95% confidence interval and the shorter error bar indicates the standard error. The dotted vertical line at 7 indicates the scale midpoint. The solid vertical line indicates the mean opinion of a promise-breaker without an excuse and the dashed line represents the mean-opinion of a non-promiser who repositioned. From the top row to the bottom, the group sizes are 70, 72, 74, 79, and 249.*

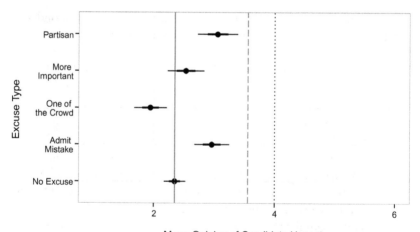

Mean Opinion of Candidate Honesty

FIGURE 7.11 Effect of excuses on candidate honesty

Note: *This figure shows the mean opinion of candidate honesty on his initial position after having broken his promise. The longer error bar indicates the 95% confidence interval and the shorter error bar indicates the standard error. The dotted vertical line at 7 indicates the scale midpoint. The solid vertical line indicates the mean opinion of a promise-breaker without an excuse, and the dashed line represents the mean opinion of a non-promiser who repositioned.*

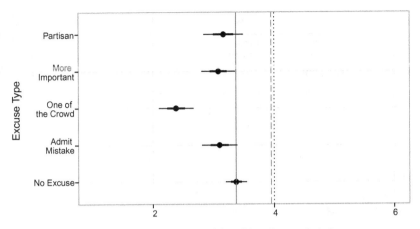

FIGURE 7.12 Effect of excuses on candidate open-mindedness

This figure shows the mean opinion of future candidate follow-through on his initial position after having broken his promise. The longer error bar indicates the 95% confidence interval and the shorter error bar indicates the standard error. The dotted vertical line at 7 indicates the scale midpoint. The solid vertical line indicates the mean opinion of a promise-breaker without an excuse, and the dashed line represents the mean opinion of a non-promiser who repositioned.

honest. In addition, these assessments are still lower than if the candidate had kept his word or if the candidate had not promised but repositioned.

Finally, Figure 7.12 shows the results of excuses on respondent opinions of candidate open-mindedness. In all cases, respondents react to the excuses by considering the candidate to be less open-minded. As with the other metrics, the "One of the Crowd" excuse is the least effective – in this case, the most damaging – while the other three excuses perform almost the same as each other. This result is unsurprising, as Chapter 5 would suggest open-mindedness and expected future follow-through have an inverse relationship. Excuses that convince the respondents that the candidate is more likely to follow through in the future are likely to also lead voters to think that the candidate is less open-minded.

Overall, these results indicate that the penalty for breaking a promise cannot be easily overcome. Excuses have some ameliorating effect, but none of the excuses improve candidate opinion so that it is as favorable as a candidate who repositions without breaking a promise. Nor do any of the excuses elevate opinions of the promiser so that it is near that of candidates who follow through on their position. Therefore, I can conclude that candidates should not make promises loosely. The harsh penalty associated with promise-breaking is not easily overcome. As a result, promises are a strong signal of candidate intention. In essence, a harsher penalty for candidates who break their word means that candidates who issue promises should be seen as more likely to follow through on their promise (as the data shows in Chapter 5).

Hillary Clinton's excuse for voting for the war in Iraq provides a good illustration of candidates' recognition of the success of excuses over the course of their career – even if she adjusted her explanation inadvertently. In the 2008 election, Hillary Clinton attempted to excuse her vote by explaining the consensus that it was the right move at the time. But in the beginnings of her bid for the 2016 election, Clinton finally admitted that she made a mistake. She changed her explanation, writing in her book, *Hard Choices,*

> [M]any Senators came to wish they had voted against the resolution. I was one of them. As the war dragged on, with every letter I sent to a family in New York who had lost a son or daughter, a father or mother, my mistake became more painful. I thought I had acted in good faith and made the best decision I could with the information I had. And I wasn't alone in getting it wrong. But I still got it wrong. Plain and simple. (Clinton, 2014)

She still invoked the "One of a Crowd" excuse, but her focus shifted almost entirely to admitting a mistake. It is impossible to tell if this issue faded because Bernie Sanders (her main opponent for the Democratic nomination) also voted similarly on war or because Clinton wisely chose admitting a mistake over the "One of a Crowd" excuse, but media questions of Clinton on the issue dissipated.

7.3 CONCLUSION

This chapter presents two studies, both of which measure the effects of acting in accordance with or against a promise with respect to acting in accordance with or against a non-promise position statement. The results in this chapter yield several important conclusions about how promises function in retrospect compared to similar statements without promises. First, promise-breakers are greatly penalized for not following through on their initial position. Second, promise-keepers are rewarded for following through on their position. In addition, promising has an effect on how respondents perceive candidates' future actions and traits. Breaking a promise causes respondents to be less certain about how a candidate will act in the future, and it also decreases respondent ratings of candidate honesty and open-mindedness. In contrast, having a promise-keeping record increases respondent perception of candidate follow-through and character. In the same way, a promise-breaking record negatively impacts opinions of candidate follow-through and character.

Finally, I demonstrate that the effects of breaking a promise are long-lasting. Candidates who break promises and make excuses never fully recover good opinions of their character or expectations that the candidate will follow through on their initial position in the future. It is difficult for a candidate to excuse inconsistency from a stated promise, a fact that helps to underscore the notion that promise-making acts as a signal for candidate action because it makes the statement more than just cheap talk.

In a book that largely focuses on the prospective effects of promise-making, this chapter may feel like a departure from the overall narrative and goal of the main theoretical argument. However, as discussed in Chapter 2, this chapter provides several important pieces of evidence for how promises matter to voters and how political theories must account for promises specifically, and various commitments made through various types of speech generally. First, promises are only compelling to voters prospectively if bad actors who depart from that signal pay a clear cost. And the evidence here indicates that voters understand promises as a signal of commitment and respond accordingly. The experiments in this chapter clearly show that there is a cost for not following through on a promise and a reward for following through on a promise. They also show that voters continue to recognize that promises are associated with an elevated sense of commitment to an issue and act accordingly. This bolsters my argument that promises continue to polarize voter opinions of candidates over non-promised positions even retrospectively. Second, this chapter affirms how critical the study of promises is to the study of representation. As Mansbridge (2003) mentions, promissory representation is an important aspect of how scholars view representation. This work underlines that it is an important aspect of how voters understand representation as well. And, it indicates that more than elected officials undertaking particularly political endeavors, voters are also very much invested in the keeping of promises themselves as a political good. Ultimately, this chapter plays a very important role in the narrative of the book underlining the three main points of this book: (1) candidates who make promises send an important signal to voters, (2) voters notice the signal from candidates, and (3) the promise signals increased commitment to an issue, which ultimately polarizes voter evaluations of candidates.

APPENDIX

7.A Full Set of Hypotheses

TABLE 7.4 *Hypothesized differences in mean opinion of a candidates*

Main Hypothesis: Voters recognize and evaluate elected official performance differently based on whether they have promised or not.

For candidates who follow through on their initial position...

1   Voters prefer candidates who promise to candidates who do not promise.

2   Following through on a promise confers higher expectations of future follow-through relative to simply following through on a non-promise position statement.

3   Promising increases ratings of honesty when compared to candidates who take the same position without promising.

4   A promiser should be viewed as less open-minded than a non-promiser.

For candidates who do not follow through on their initial position...

5   Voters prefer candidates who do not promise to candidates who promise.

6   Repositioning after promising indicates lower expectations for future follow-through relative to simply following through on a non-promise position statement.

7   Promising decreases ratings of honesty when compared to candidates who take the same position without promising.

8   A promiser should be viewed as more open-minded than a non-promiser.

Generally...

9   Candidates who follow through will be seen as more likely to follow through on their initial position in the future than candidates who reposition.

10 Candidates who follow through will be seen as more honest than candidates who reposition.

11 Promise-breaker excuses will not cause ratings of future follow-through, honesty, or open-mindedness to be as high as the ratings for a candidate who repositions but does not promise.

Note: Hypotheses 1–10 are tested by Study 1. Study 2 is a robustness check for Hypotheses 9–10, and directly tests Hypothesis 11.

TABLE 7.5 *YouGov sample, Retrospective Promise Experiment*

Demographic	Minimum	Maximum	Mean	Std. Error
Age	19.00	93.00	48.97	0.37
Female	0.00	1.00	0.53	0.01
White	0.00	1.00	0.72	0.01
Married	0.00	1.00	0.50	0.01
Party	−3.00	3.00	−0.34	0.05
Ideology	−2.00	2.00	0.09	0.02
Employment	0.00	2.00	0.85	0.02
Education	1.00	6.00	3.37	0.03
Registered voter	0.00	1.00	0.98	0.00
Interest in news	1.00	7.00	1.84	0.03

TABLE 7.6 *Mechanical Turk sample, Retrospective Promise Experiment*

Demographic	Minimum	Maximum	Mean	Std. Error
Female	0.00	1.00	0.34	0.03
White	0.00	1.00	0.80	0.02
Party	−3.00	3.00	−0.73	0.09
Education	1.00	6.00	4.13	0.07
Registered voter	0.00	1.00	0.87	0.01
Interest in news	1.00	4.00	2.17	0.05

7.B Survey Demographics

The demographics for the survey respondents are presented in Tables 7.5 and 7.6. The YouGov sample contains a more complete profile than the Mechanical Turk sample, but we can see that the sample is what we would expect from Berinsky, Huber, and Lenz (2012). Overall, the sample is more male, slightly more white, slightly more educated, and more liberal. There are fewer registered voters, but there is a greater interest in the news. Despite these differences in demographic values, the treatment groups are relatively balanced so the varying demographics should not impact the integrity of the survey experiments.

8

Promises in 2016 and beyond

The study of representation often begins with a description of the paradox that representation itself undermines democracy, the rule of the people (Manin, 1997). And yet, understanding the selection of representation is necessary to understanding how democracy functions and can succeed. While many formulations of representation exist, the dominant conception is that of promissory representation or the mandate theory of democracy (Mansbridge, 2003). Promissory representation requires attention to the candidate-positioning portion through which officials get elected (Mayhew, 2004[1974]). To date, much of the attention focuses on one of two veins: (1) how candidates position themselves to persuade voters (e.g., Tomz and Houweling, 2008) and (2) how elected officials fulfill their promises (e.g., Thomson et al., 2017). While both are important aspects of promissory representation, this book extends them by demonstrating that promises exist as a subset of issue positions and they affect voter evaluations of candidates in the process of candidate selection.

The evidence in this book has pointed repeatedly to the fact that promises matter; they are represented in candidate speech and alter voter evaluations of candidates. To underscore the first point, and draw implications for why promises should be considered in the context of campaigns, the next section will consider how promises functioned in the 2016 general election debates. This exercise demonstrates that even in an election that was strange in many ways, promises played an important role. Additionally, I examine how both presidential candidates used promises, what this may mean for strategic campaign rhetoric, and what this might suggest about how promises matter for selection of representation moving forward.

There are two critical conclusions that I highlight in closing. First, it is clear that candidates differentiate the way that they talk about issue positions, including by promising and not promising. Second, the different types of statements candidates made changed voter response to them, and voter preferences that attend to the higher commitments communicated through promises reinforced these promises. These findings have implications for both positive and normative investigations of representation and voter behavior that I discuss in this chapter. Ultimately, the data in this book has underscored that promises signal greater commitment and have a crucial effect on candidate selection.

8.1 PROMISES IN THE 2016 ELECTION

The 2016 US election saw a renewed interest in the role of rhetoric in political behavior. The focus, however, was not just on the positions that were taken but on the rhetoric that they used to make them. Work has investigated how gendered political speech may have influenced voting decisions (Bracic, Israel-Trummel, and Shortle, 2019). Other work has queried the role of racial and ethnic appeals (Strolovitch, Wong, and Proctor, 2017), particularly the role of explicit and implicit appeals in the 2016 election (Sides, Tesler, and Vavreck, 2019). Although capturing salient and distinguishing features of 2016, much of this work investigates how 2016 differed from past elections. Here, I consider how a framework of promises and commitment mattered even in the 2016 election, where rhetoric shifted substantially.

The descriptive data collection in Chapter 3 focused on elections from 1960 through 2012, and demonstrated that position-taking is a key focus of candidate speech. Importantly, these data showed that candidates address positions differently, sometimes promising and sometimes not promising. Over time, promised positions have increased, at least in presidential general election debates. Since 2016 saw differences around the unique candidacies of both party nominees, it is useful to consider how they made position statements during that time period.[1] Given these

---

[1] Clinton was the first female major party nominee for president as well as a former secretary of state and first lady. Trump, formerly not even a consistently registered Republican voter (Bump, 2015), was a surprising choice of nominee as a party outsider and because of his lack of polish. Perhaps more critical, however, was the fact that they were the most disapproved of candidates to ever run in the general presidential election (Enten, 2016).

differences, did it nonetheless reflect the trend in promising? In what ways does a more nuanced understanding of position-taking increase our understanding of candidate evaluations and representation? Here, I examine the role of rhetoric in the 2016 general election debates to examine the patterns of promised and non-promised position statements, demonstrating that the distinction in speech has continued and examining how viewing position statements in light of their commitment yields important nuances in candidate speech patterns and strategic candidate rhetoric.

8.2 POSITION-TAKING IN THE 2016 ELECTIONS

As it had since 1988, the Commission on Presidential Debates hosted three debates between candidates former Secretary of State Hillary Clinton and subsequently elected President Donald Trump. As before, each debate featured a range of topics and moderators, and also included one town hall debate featuring questions from voters in the audience.[2] As in Chapter 3, all three presidential election debates were coded by determining policy statements, and then whether the policy position was coded.[3]

8.2.1 Positions in the 2016 Debates

The debates covered a wide range of discussions, including policy topics as well as discussions of candidate qualification for office, candidate attitudes about race, and candidate character. Policy topics included questions on criminal justice, immigration, abortion, maternity leave, and foreign policy in the Middle East and with Russia. Figure 8.1 demonstrates that promised positions have continued to remain higher than non-promised positions. Both types of position statements remained more common than in 1992 and prior debate years, suggesting a continued

---

[2] The town hall debate included a new feature: a few questions submitted online by a virtual audience. Each debate ran for approximately ninety minutes. Although the percent of American adults who watch presidential debates has declined, the first debate was the most viewed debate of all time. Surpassing the 80.1 million viewers of the first 1980 presidential debate, 84 million viewers on the 13 channels broadcasting the debates and another 22.9 million streaming viewers watched Trump and Clinton. But as usual, the second and third debates saw a decline in the number of viewers, both live and streamed. For a more complete overview, see Nielsen (2016).

[3] See Chapter 3 for the coding procedure.

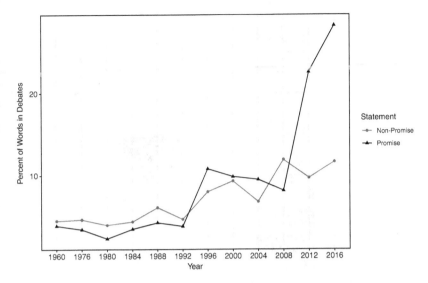

FIGURE 8.1 Promise and non-promise policy statements, 1960–2016

Note: *These results show the percent of the words within a debate that each candidate spent discussing policy as a promise or without a promise.*

change in candidate rhetoric following 1992 that was discussed in Chapter 3. This figure denotes the percent of the time the candidate spoke discussing a position, whether promised or not. This metric was chosen to consider differences in speaking time, and to better account for breaks in discussions of the same policy position by candidates.

Much public dialogue around 2016 centered on how different the candidates and the election were for every other. And there were key differences, both in the nominees and in the tenor of the rhetoric. But much of the general election dialogue continued the trajectory I describe in Chapter 3. Candidate statements included both promises and non-promise position statements. In two ways relevant to promises, the debates of 2016 continued the trends of debates past. First, this analysis of 2016 underscores that the way that candidates talk about policy is fundamentally different than in decades past. Both the ways that they speak about policy and how often they are willing to do so have changed. Second, the trend demonstrated in Chapter 3 continues here: The amount of time spent discussing a candidate's own position is higher compared to decades past. Further, in 2016 the amount of time spent promising remained higher than time spent not promising.

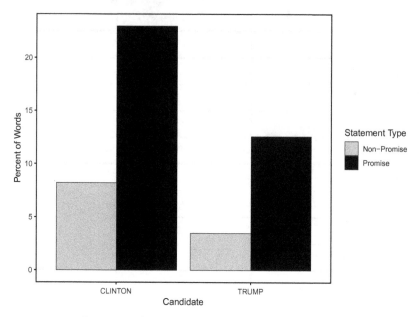

FIGURE 8.2 Promise and non-promise policy statements by candidate, 2016
Note: These results show the percent of the words within a debate that each candidate spent discussing policy as a promise or without a promise.

Figure 8.2 depicts the proportion of time that Clinton and Trump spent on the different types of campaign speech. Both candidates spent more time making promises than non-promises, though Clinton conveyed much more information through both promised and non-promised position statements than her opponent. Thus, the increase in time spent discussing policy and telling voters that they will act on those positions continued in 2016.

Clearly, conceptualizing campaign positions needs to be recognized as something more than information about where the candidate is on an ideological spectrum. As campaign research has noted, policy positions strongly affect how candidates relate to voters. Indeed, several sets of literature have developed to discuss not only how voters utilize policy positions to determine voter choice (e.g., Milita, Ryan, and Simas, 2014) but also how uncertain voters are about candidate positions (e.g., Vavreck, 2001), whether ambiguity helps or hurts candidates (e.g., VanSickle-Ward, 2014), and whether voters know enough to successfully participate in elections (e.g., Krupnikov and Ryan, 2017). Other key work leverages a different piece of why promises matter: whether or not elected officials (or parties) keep promises (Thomson et al., 2017), and why voters are skeptical of elected officials' intent to keep promises (Naurin, 2011). Collectively, an important step forward in each of these pieces is investigating a fuller set of how candidates indicate positions. This slightly shifts the focus to a paradigm to investigate how voters prioritize and give attention to different types of position statements.

8.2.2 Examining 2016 and How Candidates Use Promises

I have argued throughout this book that promises are a distinct type of position-taking, demonstrating that candidates indeed use promises and non-promise statements and voters react differently to them. A key implication of this argument is that candidates may strategically apply the use of promised and non-promised positions in different ways. A closer look at how Clinton and Trump used the different types of statements supports this claim, for four reasons.

First, both Clinton and Trump were keen to reference identifiable future actions or outcomes and promise on issues that were quite prominent in their campaigns. For instance, Trump's campaign, prominently focusing on immigration, very clearly outlined that he intended to have a border wall, as well as what outcome he hoped to achieve:

We're going to have borders in our country, which we don't have now. People are pouring into our country, and they're coming in from the Middle East and other places. We're going to make America safe again. (Trump, 2016*b*)

In addition to immigration issues and border control, arguably his core issues, Trump made promises on gun safety, removing NAFTA, draining the swamp, cutting income taxes, and import taxes, which he said he would increase in order to increase domestic jobs. Although his promises often gave few specifics on how he would enact them, his statements about policy frequently included promissory language. For instance, regarding taxes, he said, "And by the way, my tax cut is the biggest since Ronald Reagan. I'm very proud of it. It will create tremendous numbers of new jobs" (Trump, 2016*a*). This statement was typical in that it was unclear what taxes Trump would cut, but he was very clear as to its expected impact.

Similarly, Clinton made promises on her most prominent issues. These included taxes, improving the Affordable Care Act, and protecting abortion rights. For example, she was very strongly committed to defending women's health, as she said, "I will defend Planned Parenthood. I will defend Roe v. Wade, and I will defend women's rights to make their own health care decisions" (Clinton, 2016*b*). She also was far more specific in her commitments, saying she would not act in some areas of gun control and not increase particular types of taxes. For instance, "I have said repeatedly throughout this campaign: I will not raise taxes on anyone making $250, 000 or less. I also will not add a penny to the debt" (Clinton, 2016*b*).[4]

Second, both candidates spent time taking positions without making promises, though Trump spent much less time taking positions without promises than Clinton. Trump's use of non-promised positions tended to involve foreign policy: "And as far as Japan is concerned, I want to help all of our allies, but we are losing billions and billions of dollars. We cannot be the policemen of the world. We cannot protect countries all over the world" (Trump, 2016*a*).

Clinton also took positions without promises – mainly on issues that were likely to receive strong pushback from opponents of her position, such as stricter gun control and some components of her tax proposals. When she discussed repatriating money from overseas, a key policy proposal that Trump agreed with, she was much softer. Responding to his assertion about this issue, she said,

We've looked at your tax proposals. I don't see changes in the corporate tax rates or the kinds of proposals you're referring to that would cause the repatriation, bringing back of money that's stranded overseas. I happen to support that. ... I happen to support that in a way that will actually work to our benefit. (Clinton, 2016*a*)

Thus she criticized her opponent but did not respond with a strong commitment on the issue.

Third, in 2016, promissory language (statements that explicitly say "I promise," or similar phrases) entered the debates in connection with Clinton's discussions on race and policy, though they appeared less directly in other types of policy statements. Given that the 2016 election in large part centered on Trump's derisive language toward immigrants, refugees, African Americans, and women (even during the general election debates), Clinton was keen to demonstrate both her commitment

---

[4] The contrast between this statement and Trump's also suggests the strategic use of promises in conjunction with ambiguity. Perhaps a demonstration of higher commitment may combine with more ambiguous language to be appealing to key voters.

to equity and inclusiveness and Trump's failures (Sides, Tesler, and Vavreck, 2019). As a result, in multiple instances, she invoked promissory language:

If we set those goals and we go together to try to achieve them, there's nothing in my opinion that America can't do. So that's why I hope that we will come together in this campaign. Obviously, I'm hoping to earn your vote, I'm hoping to be elected in November, and I can promise you, I will work with every American. I want to be the president for all Americans, regardless of your political beliefs, where you come from, what you look like, your religion. (Clinton, 2016c)

No doubt, Clinton's goal here is not only to endorse positions that will benefit Black and Latinx voters but also to indicate that these were serious commitments she intended to center as president and to assure other voters she would reach across the aisle.

Finally, there were key rhetorical differences in how both candidates used promises. As evidenced in Figure 8.2, Trump spent less time taking positions, whether promised or not. It is difficult to determine if this resulted simply from speaking style or due to experience and a targeted campaign strategy. Certainly some of the difference in the time the candidates spent promising was due to the rambling nature of Trump's responses. For instance, moderator Lester Holt asked, "You've talked about creating 25 million jobs, and you've promised to bring back millions of jobs for Americans. How are you going to bring back the industries that have left this country for cheaper labor overseas?" And Trump responded,

Well, for one thing – and before we start on that – my father gave me a very small loan in 1975, and I built it into a company that's worth many, many billions of dollars, with some of the greatest assets in the world, and I say that only because that's the kind of thinking that our country needs. Our country's in deep trouble. We don't know what we're doing when it comes to devaluations and all of these countries all over the world, especially China. They're the best, the best ever at it. What they're doing to us is a very, very sad thing. So we have to do that. (Trump, 2016a)

Amid this type of language, Trump sometimes skirted policy discussions with either tangentially relevant information or by obscurely referencing another government's action or plan (generally without any specifics). As in this statement, he did both. He also interjected quite often during Clinton's speech (so much so that multiple moderators admonished him to be quiet), and attacked her record or other Democrat records (especially that of Barack Obama and Bill Clinton). A more practiced and polished public speaker, Clinton sidestepped direct questions differently than Trump, but she still did not directly address policy if she did not want to. At these points, she attacked her opponent's positions or record.

Clinton also used promissory language to help distinguish herself from Trump as well as to indicate her intent to maintain the status quo on international relations.

> Words matter when you run for president. And they really matter when you are president. And I want to reassure our allies in Japan and South Korea and elsewhere that we have mutual defense treaties and we will honor them. It is essential that America's word be good. And so I know that this campaign has caused some questioning and some worries on the part of many leaders across the globe. I've talked with a number of them. But I want to – on behalf of myself, and I think on behalf of a majority of the American people – say that, you know, our word is good. (Clinton, 2016a)

In another case, on a position unpopular with Republicans, Clinton combined a promise to do something with a promise to maintain the status quo. For example, Clinton is adamant that

> I am on record as saying that we need to put more money into the Social Security Trust Fund. That's part of my commitment to raise taxes on the wealthy. My Social Security payroll contribution will go up, as will Donald's, assuming he can't figure out how to get out of it. But what we want to do is to replenish the Social Security Trust Fund ... by making sure that we have sufficient resources, and that will come from either raising the cap and/or finding other ways to get more money into it. I will not cut benefits. (Clinton, 2016b)

This statement may represent intentionally recognizing the smaller power of appealing on a status quo issue, demonstrated in Chapter 5 and in Kostadinova (2013), Royed (1996), Costello and Thomson (2008) and Thomson (2001).

Both candidates clearly demonstrated differences in the ways that they took positions on different issues. On issues that were central to their campaigns, the language signaled a promise and commitment to act or to achieve an outcome. On issues that were less important to their campaigns, the candidates were likely to either sidestep or discuss their positions with much less force, typically indicating their beliefs or support or opposition but not indicating if it was something they would acted on in office. A closer look at the 2016 promises indicates that candidates spoke about policy through both promises and non-promises, much as they have in debates past. It also demonstrates that promises appear to be a strategic rhetorical device, used consistently

with how voters viewed promises in Chapter 4 as a way for candidates
to signal commitment to voters.

8.3 PROMISES AND NORMATIVE THEORY

All of the data in this book, including the examples from 2016, indicates
that what it means for candidates to make a promise should be concep-
tualized differently in normative theory and promissory representation.
Conceptions of representation summarize empirical studies and drive
future investigations of political representation. Promises deserve a
second glance based on the findings here because position statements
are not only recognized differently by candidates but also responded to
differently by voters. Moving forward, normative theories of promissory
representation need to reflect the influence of promises and perceived
commitment on voter decision-making as well as voters' perception
of the importance of promise-keeping versus attachment to actualized
positions.

First, because promises are a distinct form of policy statements and
probably an important strategic element in campaigns, normative theory
must leave room for these variations in prospective speech. Current
theory tends to view promissory representation as simplistic; voters
are attracted by candidate positions and assess those positions to make
decisions. While the experiments here demonstrate that it is true, they also
demonstrate that voters react differently to promises, as demonstrated in
Chapters 5 and 6 and in the 2016 debates. This suggests that, more than
simply noticing positions, voters notice perceived commitment to those
positions. Normative theory needs to consider commitment to campaign
positions and not simply the positions themselves. This also includes
slightly higher attraction to candidates who promise, but perhaps more
importantly, the stronger repelling effect of promises when voters and
candidates do not align on promised positions. As theory accounts for
candidate strategy, it should also consider how promises play into both
of these types of roles. Because the repelling effect of disagreeing with a
promise is so strong, there is a need to account for how candidates may
limit their appeals to prevent further costs among the opposition.

Second, the retrospective experiments in Chapter 7 clearly suggest that
voters so strongly identify with the norms of candidates following through
on promises that they both rank and rate elected officials who break their
promises more harshly even when the elected officials act as the voters

would want them to. It is somewhat surprising to see instances where voters prioritized regulating promise-breaking over their own preferred positions, but it speaks to the critical importance to the standards of accountability and how voters define good representation (Dovi, 2012). An important exercise for normative theory would be to consider the instances in which promises matter more than positions themselves, and how these may alter voter perceptions of candidate selection as well as accountability.

8.4 PROMISES AND VOTER BEHAVIOR

A second goal of this book was to determine if promises mattered for voter assessments of candidates, particularly with respect to similar, non-promised positions. Promises unequivocally increased voter perceptions of candidates' commitment to their stated policy positions, as demonstrated in Chapter 4. Similarly, promises increased voters' perception of the likelihood that the candidate will work to achieve the policy they propose, although promises do not change voter perceptions that candidates will successfully realize a shift in actual policy once in office. Despite increased levels of commitment that promises suggest, voters penalize promisers with perceptions of lower levels of character, measured here by honesty and open-mindedness in Chapter 5. These two evaluations seem to lead to conflicting outcomes for how promises affect voter perceptions based on whether voter positions align with the candidate's or not. Because when voter positions align with the candidate's and the candidate would act in accordance with the voter's preferences, candidates who promise were preferred. The conflicting negatives that promises induce due to candidate character seem to decrease how positively voters view promises. Alternatively, when voter positions do not align with candidate preferences, voters perceive promising quite negatively because the candidates are committing to a position with which the voters disagree, thus decreasing evaluations of candidate character. Quite clearly, promises polarize evaluations of candidates. And promises polarize evaluations not just prospectively but retrospectively as well, suggesting that voters do consider campaign commitments to issues to matter in the assessment of elected official success.

   That promises matter to voters is clear from this data, and intersects with other important questions in political science. Consider how promises may link to other important questions in investigations, including polarization in the US context. It is widely confirmed that elites in American politics are polarized, and increasingly so (Hetherington, 2001). It is somewhat contested whether the American public is similarly polarized, with one camp arguing that the public is polarizing to match party elites (Abramowitz and Saunders, 2008) and the other camp arguing that what appears to be polarization is actually partisan sorting (Fiorina and Abrams, 2008; Fiorina and Levendusky, 2006). The focus in this debate is how wide the actual distance is between positions in the two parties. However, regardless of real differences between the two parties, the perceived difference between them seems to be growing more pronounced (Westfall et al., 2015; Ahler and Sood, 2018), and other indicators seem to have polarized as well, including trust in government (Hetherington and Rudolph, 2015). Perhaps, more importantly, more negative perceptions of the other party may induce a growing divide in affect toward the other party (Mason, 2018). The data and arguments illustrated here indicate that, in this larger context, it is important to consider the types of policy statements that candidates are making to voters. By inducing greater levels of commitment, candidates are polarizing attitudes about themselves to voters and may, in fact, be reinforcing distance – real or perceived – between partisan voters. Most striking from the data here is that promises instill a much more negative reaction than positive reaction from voters.

This work helps both to illuminate and refocus investigator understanding for how voters conceive campaign promises. An important puzzle in the literature investigating promises – called the "pledge paradox" – has been why voters anticipate that candidates will break their promises even when empirical evidence demonstrates that candidates are prone to keep them (Thomson et al., 2017). Interviews with voters indicate that, as with scholars, there are significant disagreements about what it means to fulfill a promise (Naurin, 2014). However, reaching a consensus on what fulfillment means and whether fulfillment is achieved may not be the only decision points with which voters grapple. Especially since voters use information about candidates as signals for how those candidates will behave in office (Fearon, 1999),[5] it is important to consider this

---

[5] This suggests that the retrospective focus on promises, while important for thinking about accountability and outcomes for implications of promissory representation or the mandate theory of democracy, cannot tell the whole story. Signals are prospective considerations of future actions. As such, the work I have done here to measure promises prospectively is a necessary and critical contribution.

paradox prospectively. The work in Chapters 5 and 6 indicates that voters are not simply grappling with how past officials or parties have fulfilled promises; voters also use position statements (promises or not) to make judgments about candidates' future actions and character. That Chapter 5 demonstrates that voters do not necessarily expect candidates who follow through to also be honest indicates the doubt voters have about promise fulfillment. The Oversaturation Experiment in Chapter 6 further suggests that the conflict is not simply about doubt regarding candidate actions, because Chapters 4 and 5 tell us that promises heighten expectations of action and commitment, but also about doubt over candidate success at achieving policy outcomes. Considering the voter's motivations from this perspective, the puzzle is not one about voter expectations for action but instead about voter expectations for policy realization.

Finally, this work has made clear that the elevated level of commitment to an issue factors into retrospective voter judgments of candidates. Not only do voters prefer elected officials who followed through on campaign promises, but they also strongly dislike elected officials who break their promises. And, respondents paid more attention to whether promises were fulfilled than to the actual action taken by the candidates – meaning that voters rewarded promisers even when they disagreed with both their position and their actions. While the bulk of my argument has focused on how promises matter prospectively for voter behavior and why we need to pay attention to them, the results on how promises matter are of critical importance to that argument. That promises continue to elevate expectations for specific actions even after candidates have acted reinforces the level of perceived commitment associated with promises when they are made. In order for promises to send a signal of commitment, candidates must anticipate paying a high cost for breaking them. The data in Chapter 7 indicated that voters do negatively associate broken promises with decreased likelihood to follow through on positions in the future as well as decreased honesty and open-mindedness, and they are less likely to select a candidate who has broken a promise. Work on promise fulfillment to date has set out to determine whether promises have been fulfilled and what institutional circumstances correlate with promise fulfillment (Mansergh and Thomson, 2007). While the goal of these studies is to affirm the mandate aspect of promissory representation, they do not consider how promise fulfillment affects voter continued support (or opposition) to candidates. A final point is voters prefer candidates who act according to their promises above the actual actions on the policy. This is demonstrated in Chapter 7 that voters prefer

non-promisers over promisers even when the promisers break their word
to vote in accordance with respondent preferences. The finding is both
surprising and indicative of the importance of the promissory model
of democracy to voters, when taking into account varying levels of
commitment in candidate positions.

8.5 PROMISES AND CAMPAIGNS

Finally, it is just as important to consider what a more nuanced understanding of promises implies for campaign strategy. In Chapter 3 and
earlier in this chapter, I demonstrate that candidates do vary position
statements in US presidential general election debates. While the data
here is limited to statements in the debates, the results should translate
to other levels of government and other political forums. As Petrocik
(1996) explains, representation of the issues that candidates discuss is
quite consistent across mode of speech (stump speeches, advertisements,
and debates). And, candidate motivations appear to be similar across
electoral level – to get elected and stay in office. That the variance exists
indicates what might be a strategic decision to appeal to supporters.

Riker (1996) argued that the strategy of political rhetoric and its power
to persuade was not well understood – and how promises matter is a
novel contribution to this discussion. Understanding how promises affect
voters and the frequency with which candidates use them indicates that
promises have value in persuading voters of the candidate's commitment
to the issue and clarifying uncertainty about what the candidate would
do on that issue. (Campaigns can affect voters through agenda-setting,
persuading, and clarifying; promises might affect voters through the later
two mechanisms and may signal the first. See Vavreck (2009).) Candidates spend time defending themselves on positions and working to convince voters that they are committed to advancing voters' interests (Fenno,
2004[1973]; Sulkin, 2011). Just as candidates establish authority and
trust by invoking their records, promises are a tool with which candidates
indicate commitment, as Clinton and Trump did highlighting their key
issues in 2016. As a result, studies of candidate positions and campaign
strategy need to account for them.

That the number of promises have increased in the American context means that attention to promises is quite timely. This finding also
agrees with findings of increases in promises in party manifestos world-
wide. The number of party pledges have increased over the past thirty
years in Ireland, the Netherlands, and Spain (Thomson, 2001; Mansergh

and Thomson, 2007; Artes, 2011; Håkansson and Naurin, 2016). This increase in promises seems to be a strategic calculation and an attempt to capture a greater media spotlight (Håkansson and Naurin, 2016), which differentially highlights various aspects of promises (Kostadinova, 2015). In the American context presented in Chapter 3, the increase in promises began after 1992, a time when campaigns drastically changed how candidates interacted with the media (Baum and Kernell, 1999; Baum, 2005). Because media gives more attention to promises, candidates may have more incentive to make them (Kostadinova, 2015).

Promises clearly establish a greater sense of candidate commitment to an issue. As such, promising helps to address the problem of position-taking inherent by creating a stronger signal that the candidate intends to do what the candidate says. However, promising is not without draw-backs – both strategic for the candidate and of concern to constituents. Promising significantly decreases voters' perceptions of candidates' character (which they may be able to alleviate by following through once in office). For voters, promises tend to cause candidates to be viewed as more entrenched in and committed to their positions, and less flexible to accommodate changes in constituent preferences. And, for the whole political system, promises seem to cause (or reinforce) a polarized impression of elites. That promises have wide-reaching effects at all levels of politics is a compelling reason to continue accounting for them in studies of representation.

Bibliography

Abramowitz, A. I., and K. L. Saunders. 2008. "Is Polarization a Myth?" *The Journal of Politics* 70 (2): 542–555.

Adams, J., L. Ezrow, and Z. Somer-Topcu. 2011. "Is Anybody Listening? Evidence That Voters Do Not Respond to European Parties' Policy Statements during Elections." *American Journal of Political Science* 55 (2): 370–382.

2014. "Do Voters Respond to Party Manifestos or to a Wider." *American Journal of Political Science* 58 (4): 967–978.

Ahler, D. J., and G. Sood. 2018. "The Parties in Our Heads: Misperceptions about Party Composition and Their Consequences." *The Journal of Politics* 80 (3): 964–981.

Aldrich, J. H. 1995. *Why Parties?: The Origin and Transformation of Political Parties in America.* Chicago: University of Chicago Press.

Alesina, A., and A. Cukierman. 1990. "The Politics of Ambiguity." *The Quarterly Journal of Economics* 105 (4): 829–850.

Allgeier, A., D. Byrne, B. Brooks, and D. Revnes. 1979. "The Waffle Phenomenon: Negative Evaluations of Those Who Shift Attitudinally." *Journal of Applied Social Psychology* 9 (2): 170–182.

Alston, L. J., and B. Mueller. 2006. "Pork for Policy: Executive and Legislative Exchange in Brazil." *Journal of Law, Economics, and Organization* 22 (1): 87–114.

Alvarez, R. M. 1997. *Information and Elections.* Ann Arbor: University of Michigan Press.

Alvarez, R. M., and C. H. Franklin. 1994. "Uncertainty and Political Perceptions." *The Journal of Politics* 56 (3): 671–688.

Anderson, S. E., D. M. Butler, and L. Harbridge-Yong. 2020. *Rejecting Compromise: Legislators' Fear of Primary Voters.* Cambridge: Cambridge University Press.

ANES. 2012. "The ANES 2012 Times Series Study." *American National Election Studies.* https://electionstudies.org/data-center/2012-time-series-study/ (accessed: November 10, 2014).

Ansolabehere, S., and S. Iyengar. 1994. "Riding the Wave and Claiming Ownership over Issues: The Joint Effects of Advertising and News Coverage in Campaigns." *Public Opinion Quarterly* 58 (3): 335–357.

Aragones, E., A. Postlewaite, and T. Palfrey. 2007. "Political Reputations and Campaign Promises." *Journal of the European Economic Association* 5 (4): 846–884.

Artes, J. 2011. "Do Spanish Politicians Keep Their Promises?" *Party Politics* 19 (1): 142–158.

Austen-Smith, D., and J. Banks. 1989. "Electoral Accountability and Incumbency." In *Models of Strategic Choice in Politics*, ed. P. Ordeshook. Ann Arbor: University of Michigan Press, chapter 7, 121–148.

Austin, J. L. 1975. *How to Do Things with Words*, vol. 1955. Oxford: Oxford University Press.

Azari, J. R. 2014. *Delivering the People's Message: The Changing Politics of the Presidential Mandate*. Ithaca, NY: Cornell University Press.

Azevedo, F., J. T. Jost, and T. Rothmund. 2017. "Making America Great Again: System Justification in the US Presidential Election of 2016." *Translational Issues in Psychological Science* 3 (3): 231.

Baker, P. 2008. "Obama Team Weighs What to Take on First." www.nytimes .com/2008/11/09/us/politics/09promises.html?searchResultPosition=9 (published March 18, 2015; accessed June 27, 2020).

Banks, J. S. 1990. "A Model of Electoral Competition with Incomplete Information." *Journal of Economic Theory* 50 (2): 309–325.

Baron, D. P. 1989. "Service-Induced Campaign Contributions and the Electoral Equilibrium." *The Quarterly Journal of Economics* 104 (1): 45–72.

Bartels, L. M. 1986. "Issue Voting under Uncertainty: An Empirical Test." *American Journal of Political Science* 30 (4): 709–728.

Baum, M. A. 2005. "Talking the Vote: Why Presidential Candidates Hit the Talk Show Circuit." *American Journal of Political Science* 49 (2): 213–234.

Baum, M. A., and S. Kernell. 1999. "Has Cable Ended the Golden Age of Presidential Television?" *American Political Science Review* 93 (1): 99–114.

BBC. 2013. "Gabrielle Giffords Launches Gun Control Campaign." www.bbc .com/news/world-us-canada-20949405. (accessed April 1, 2014)

Benoit, W. L. 2000. "A Functional Analysis of Political Advertising across Media, 1998." *Communication Studies* 51 (3): 274–295.

——— 2004. "Political Party Affiliation and Presidential Campaign Discourse." *Communication Quarterly* 52 (2): 81–97.

Berinsky, A. J., and J. B. Lewis. 2007. "An Estimate of Risk Aversion in the US Electorate." *Quarterly Journal of Political Science* 2 (2): 139–154.

Berinsky, A. J., G. A. Huber, and G. S. Lenz. 2012. "Evaluating Online Labor Markets for Experimental Research: Amazon's Mechanical Turk." *Political Analysis* 20 (3): 351–368.

Bianco, W. T. 1994. *Trust: Representatives and Constituents*. Ann Arbor: University of Michigan Press.

Borunda, D., and M. Mekelburg. 2018. "Ted Cruz Wins Texas Senate Race, but Beto O'Rourke Draws All Eyes to El Pasol." www.elpasotimes.com/story/news/politics/elections/2018/11/06/ted-cruz-wins-texas-senate-race-beto-orourke-draws-eyes-el-paso/1905477002/ (published November 6, 2018; accessed November 6, 2018).

Bracic, A., M. Israel-Trummel, and A. F. Shortle. 2019. "Is Sexism for White People? Gender Stereotypes, Race, and the 2016 Presidential Election." *Political Behavior* 41 (2): 281–307.

Bradley, J. P. 1969. "Party Platforms & Party Performance Concerning Social Security." *Polity* 1 (3): 337–358.

Brady, H. E., and S. Ansolabehere. 1989. "The Nature of Utility Functions in Mass Publics." *American Political Science Review* 83 (1): 143–163.

Brazeal, L. M., and W. L. Benoit. 2001. "A Functional Analysis of Congressional Television Spots, 1986–2000." *Communication Quarterly* 49 (4): 436–454.

Buehler, R., D. Griffin, and M. Ross. 1994. "Exploring the 'Planning Fallacy': Why People Underestimate Their Task Completion Times." *Journal of Personality and Social Psychology* 67 (3): 366.

Bühlmann, M., A. F. Widmer, and L. Schädel. 2010. "Substantive and Descriptive Representation in Swiss Cantons." *Swiss Political Science Review* 16 (3): 565–595.

Bullock, J. G., and S. E. Ha. 2011. "Mediation Analysis Is Harder than It Looks." *Cambridge Handbook of Experimental Political Science*, eds. J. Druckman, D. P. Green, J. H. Kuklinski, and A. Lupia. New York: Cambridge University Press, 508–521.

Bump, P. 2015. "Donald Trumps Got a Particularly Strange Voting History." www.washingtonpost.com/news/the-fix/wp/2015/11/07/donald-trumps-got-a-particularly-strange-voting-history/ (accessed November 7, 2018).

——— 2016. "Donald Trump Took 5 Different Positions on Abortion in 3 Days." www.washingtonpost.com/news/the-fix/wp/2016/04/03/donald-trumps-ever-shifting-positions-on-abortion/?utm_term=.ce30842939ca (accessed November 7, 2017).

Burden, B. 2007. *The Personal Roots of Representation*. Princeton: University of Princeton Press.

Burke, E. 1987. "Speech to the Electors of Bristol on Being Elected (Nov. 1774)." In *The Political Philosophy of Edmund Burke*, ed. I. Hampsher-Monk. London: Longman, 108–111.

Bush, G. H. W. 1988. "The Presidential Debate; Transcript of the Second Debate between Bush and Dukakis." www.nytimes.com/1988/10/14/us/the-presidential-debate-transcript-of-the-second-debate-between-bush-and-dukakis.html (accessed February 23, 2012).

——— 1992. "Presidential Debate in Richmond, Virginia on October 15." *The American Presidency Project*.

——— 2004. "Presidential Debate in St. Louis, Missouri on October 8." *The American Presidency Project*.

Cain, B., J. Ferejohn, and M. Fiorina. 1987. *The Personal Vote: Constituency Service and Electoral Independence*. Cambridge, MA: Harvard University Press.

Callander, S. 2008a. "A Theory of Policy Expertise." *Quarterly Journal of Political Science* 3 (May 2007): 123–140.

2008b. "Political Motivations." *Review of Economic Studies* 75 (3): 671–697.

Callander, S., and S. Wilkie. 2007. "Lies, Damned Lies, and Political Campaigns." *Games and Economic Behavior* 60 (2): 262–286.

Callander, S., and C. H. Wilson. 2008. "Context Dependent Voting and Political Ambiguity." *Journal of Public Economics* 92 (3): 565–581.

Calvert, R. L. 1985. "Robustness of the Multidimensional Voting Model: Candidate Motivations, Uncertainty, and Convergence." *American Journal of Political Science* 29 (1): 69–95.

Campbell, J. E. 1983. "The Electoral Consequences of Issue Ambiguity: An Examination of the Presidential Candidates' Issue Positions from 1968 to 1980." *Political Behavior* 5 (3): 277–291.

Canes-Wrone, B., M. C. Herron, and K. W. Shotts. 2001. "Leadership and Pandering: A Theory of Executive Policymaking." *American Journal of Political Science* 45 (3): 532–550.

Carlin, D. B. 2009. *The Third Agenda in US Presidential Debates: Debate Watch and Viewer Reactions, 1996–2004*. Westport, CT: Praeger Publishers.

Carlson, J. M., and K. Dolan. 1985. "The Waffle Phenomenon and Candidates' Image." *Psychological Reports* 57 (3): 795–798.

Charness, G., and M. Dufwenberg. 2006. "Promises and Partnership." *Econometrica* 74 (6): 1579–1601.

Charness, G., and M. Dufwenberg. 2010. "Bare Promises: An Experiment." *Economics Letters* 107 (2): 281–283.

Chong, D., and J. N. Druckman. 2011. "Identifying Frames in Political News." In *SourceBook for Political Communication Research: Methods, Measures, and Analytical Techniques*, eds. Erik P. Bucy and R. Lance Holbert. New York: Routledge, 238–267.

Clinton, B. 1991. "Announcement Speech in Little Rock, Arkansas." www.4president.org/speeches/1992/billclinton1992announcement.htm (accessed November 7, 2018).

Clinton, H. R. 2004. "Hillary Clinton: No Regret on Iraq Vote." www.cnn.com/2004/ALLPOLITICS/04/21/iraq.hillary/ (accessed July 20, 2014).

2014. *Hard Choices*, 1st ed. New York: Simon and Schuster.

2016a. "Presidential Debate in Hempstead, New York on September 26." *The New York Times*. www.nytimes.com/2012/10/16/us/politics/transcript-of-the-second-presidential-debate-in-hempstead-ny.htm (accessed January 16, 2020).

2016b. "Presidential Debate in Las Vegas, Nevada on October 19." *The New York Times*. www.nytimes.com/2016/10/20/us/politics/third-debate-transcript.html (accessed January 16, 2020).

2016c. "Presidential Debate in St. Louis, Missouri on October 9." *The New York Times*. https://www.nytimes.com/2016/09/27/us/politics/transcript-debate.html (accessed January 16, 2020).

Cobb, M. D., and J. H. Kuklinski. 1997. "Changing Minds: Political Arguments and Political Persuasion." *American Journal of Political Science* 41 (1): 88–121.

Collins, S. 2016. "All the Times Obama Has Said He's Going to Close Guantanamo Bay." https://qz.com/623131/all-the-times-obama-has-said-hes-going-to-close-guantanamo-bay/ (published February 23, 2016; accessed June 27, 2020).

Converse, P. E. 2006. "The Nature of Belief Systems in Mass Publics (1964)." *Critical Review* 18 (1–3): 1–74.

Cornyn, J. 2002. "Texas Senate Debate." www.c-span.org/video/?173416-1/texas-senate-debate&start=2196 (accessed November 7, 2018).

Costello, R., and R. Thomson. 2008. "Election Pledges and Their Enactment in Coalition Governments: A Comparative Analysis of Ireland." *Journal of Elections, Public Opinion and Parties* 18 (3): 239–256.

Craighill, P. M., and S. Clement. 2015. "Trump's Popularity Spikes among Republicans." *Washington Post.* www.washingtonpost.com/news/the-fix/wp/2015/07/15/trumps-popularity-spikes-among-republicans/ (published July 17, 2015; accessed August 2, 2015).

Debate. 1976. "Presidential Debate in Williamsburg on October 22." *The American Presidency Project.* www.presidency.ucsb.edu/documents/presidential-campaign-debate-0 (accessed February 23, 2012).

1992. "Presidential Debate in Richmond, Virginia on October 15." *The American Presidency Project.* www.presidency.ucsb.edu/documents/presidential-debate-the-university-richmond (accessed February 23, 2012).

2012. "Full Transcript of the Second Presidential Debate." *New York Times.* www.nytimes.com/2012/10/16/us/politics/transcript-of-the-second-presidential-debate-in-hempstead-ny.html (accessed August 20, 2013).

DelReal, J. A. 2016. "Trump Draws Fire for Saying Abortion Laws Are Set, 'We have to leave it that way'." Washington Post. www.washingtonpost.com/politics/trump-says-us-abortion-laws-are-set-and-we-have-to-leave-it-that-way/2016/04/02/ (published April 2, 2016; accessed November 7, 2017).

Dimitrova, D. V., and P. Kostadinova. 2013. "Identifying Antecedents of the Strategic Game Frame: A Longitudinal Analysis." *Journalism & Mass Communication Quarterly* 90 (1): 75–88.

Ditto, P. H., and A. J. Mastronarde. 2009. "The Paradox of the Political Maverick." *Journal of Experimental Social Psychology* 45 (1): 295–298.

Dixon, T. 2016. "Souh Carolina Senate Debate." www.c-span.org/video/?417499-1/south-carolina-senate-debate&start=1016 (accessed November 7, 2018).

Dovi, S. 2012. *The Good Representative*, vol. 8 John Wiley & Sons.

2018. "Political Representation." In *The Stanford Encyclopedia of Philosophy*, Winter 2017 ed. E. N. Zalta. plato.stanford.edu/archives/fall2018/entries/political-representation/ (accessed March 11, 2021).

Downs, A. 1965[1957]. *An Economic Theory of Democracy*. New York: Harper and Row.

Druckman, J. N., and C. D. Kam. 2011. "Students as Experimental Participants." *Cambridge Handbook of Experimental Political Science* 1: 41–57.

Druckman, J. N., and T. J. Leeper. 2012. "Is Public Opinion Stable? Resolving the Micro/Macro Disconnect in Studies of Public Opinion." *Daedalus* 141 (4): 50–68.

Druckman, J. N., M. J. Kifer, and M. Parkin. 2009. "Campaign Communications in US Congressional Elections." *American Political Science Review* 103 (3): 343–366.

2014. "US Congressional Campaign Communications in an Internet Age." *Journal of Elections, Public Opinion & Parties* 24 (1): 20–44.

Eaton, J. 2016. "Where Hillary Clinton and Donald Trump Stand on LGBTQ Rights." www.teenvogue.com/story/hillary-clinton-donald-trump-lgbt-lgbtq-rights-2016-election (accessed November 7, 2017).

Elinder, M., H. Jordahl, and P. Poutvaara. 2015. "Promises, Policies and Pocketbook Voting." *European Economic Review* 75: 177–194.

Enten, H. 2016. "Americans Distaste for Both Trump and Clinton Is Record-Breaking." https://fivethirtyeight.com/features/americans-distaste-for-both-trump-and-clinton-is-record-breaking/ (accessed November 7, 2018).

Erikson, R. S., and C. Wlezien. 2012. *The Timeline of Presidential Elections: How Campaigns Do (and Do Not) Matter*. Chicago: University of Chicago Press.

Fearon, J. D. 1999. "Electoral Accountability and the Control of Politicians: Selecting Good Types versus Sanctioning Poor Performance." *Democracy, Accountability, and Representation* 55: 61.

Fenno, R. F. 2004[1973]. *Congressmen in Committees*. Boston: Little Brown.

Fernandez, M. 2018. "Ted Cruz Defeats Beto O'Rourke for Senate in Texas." www.nytimes.com/2018/11/06/us/ted-cruz-wins-texas-senate-race.html (published November 6, 2018; accessed November 6, 2018).

Fiorina, M. P. 1974. *Representatives, Roll Calls, and Constituencies*. Lexington, MA: Lexington Books.

Fiorina, M. P., and S. J. Abrams. 2008. "Political Polarization in the American Public." *Annual Review of Political Science* 11: 563–588.

Fiorina, M. P., and M. S. Levendusky. 2006. "Disconnected: The Political Class versus the People." *Red and Blue Nation* 1: 49–71.

Fishel, J. 1985. *Presidents and Promises: From Campaign Pledge to Presidential Performance*. Washington, DC: CQ Press.

Ford, G. 1976a. "Presidential Debate in Philadelphia on September 23." www.presidency.ucsb.edu/ws/index.php?pid=6517; (accessed February 23, 2012).

1976b. "Presidential Debate in Williamsburg on October 22." www.presidency.ucsb.edu/ws/index.php?pid=6517; (accessed February 23, 2012).

Fox, J., and L. Rothenberg. 2011. "Influence without Bribes: A Noncontracting Model of Campaign Giving and Policymaking." *Political Analysis* mpro16.

Funk, C. L. 1996. "The Impact of Scandal on Candidate Evaluations: An Experimental Test of the Role of Candidate Traits." *Political Behavior* 18 (1): 1–24.

1999. "Bringing the Candidate into Models of Candidate Evaluation." *The Journal of Politics* 61 (3): 700–720.

Gallup. 2014. "Guns." www.gallup.com/poll/1645/guns.aspx (accessed November 10, 2014).

Geer, J. G. 2006. *In Defense of Negativity: Attack Ads in Presidential Campaigns.* Chicago: University of Chicago Press.

Glazer, A. 1990. "The Strategy of Candidate Ambiguity." *American Political Science Review* 84 (1): 237–241.

Gneezy, A., and N. Epley. 2014. "Worth Keeping but Not Exceeding: Asymmetric Consequences of Breaking versus Exceeding Promises." *Social Psychological and Personality Science* 5 (7): 796–804.

GOP. 2016. "A Better Way: Our Vision for a Confident America." www.novoco .com/sites/default/files/atoms/files/ryan_a_better_way_policy_paper_062416 .pdf (published June 24, 2016; accessed June 27, 2020).

Gore, A. 2000. "Presidential Debate in St. Louis, Missouri on October 17." *Comission on Presidential Debates.*

Goren, P. 1997. "Political Expertise and Issue Voting in Presidential Elections." *Political Research Quarterly* 50 (2): 387–412.

2007. "Character Weakness, Partisan Bias, and Presidential Evaluation: Modifications and Extensions." *Political Behavior* 29 (3): 305–325.

Gottfried, J., M. Barthel, E. Shearer, and A. Mitchell. 2016. "The 2016 Presidential Campaign – A News Event That's Hard to Miss." www.journalism.org/ 2016/02/04/the-2016-presidential-campaign-a-news-event-thats-hard-to-miss/ (published February 4, 2016; accessed June 27, 2020).

Green, J. 2007. "When Voters and Parties Agree: Valence Issues and Party Competition." *Political Studies* 55 (3): 629–655.

Grice, H. P. 1991. *Studies in the Way of Words.* Cambridge, MA: Harvard University Press.

Grimmer, J. 2013. *Representational Style in Congress: What Legislators Say and Why It Matters.* New York: Cambridge University Press.

Grimmer, J., and B. M. Stewart. 2013. "Text as Data: The Promise and Pitfalls of Automatic Content Analysis Methods for Political Texts." *Political Analysis* 21 (3): 267–297.

Grimmer, J., S. J. Westwood, and S. Messing. 2014. *The Impression of Influence: Legislator Communication, Representation, and Democratic Accountability.* Princeton, NJ: Princeton University Press.

Grofman, B. 1985. "The Neglected Role of the Status Quo in Models of Issue Voting." *The Journal of Politics* 47 (1): 229–237.

2004. "Downs and Two-Party Convergence." *Annual Review Political Science* 7: 25–46.

Grose, C. R., and J. Husser. 2014. "Is Candidate Rhetorical Tone Associated with Presidential Vote Choice?" In *Communication and Language Analysis in the Public Sphere*, ed. R. P. Hart. Hershey, PA: Information Science Review, 153–170.

Groseclose, T. 2001. "A Model of Candidate Location When One Candidate Has a Valence Advantage." *American Journal of Political Science* 45 (4): 862–886.

Grossman, G. M., and E. Helpman. 2005. "Party Discipline and Pork Barrel Politics." (No. w11396). National Bureau of Economic Research.

Hainmueller, J., and D. J. Hopkins. 2012. The Hidden American Immigration Consensus: A Conjoint Analysis of Attitudes toward Immigrants. *American Journal of Political Science* 59 (3): 529–548.

Hainmueller, J., D. J. Hopkins, and T. Yamamoto. 2014. "Causal Inference in Conjoint Analysis: Understanding Multidimensional Choices via Stated Preference Experiments." *Political Analysis* 22 (1): 1–30.

Håkansson, N., and E. Naurin 2016. "Promising Ever More." *Party Politics* 22 (3): 393–404.

Hall, R. 1996. *Participation in Congress.* New Haven: Yale University Press.

Harrington, J. E. 1993. "Economic Policy, Economic Performance, and Elections." *The American Economic Review* 83 (1): 27–42.

Hetherington, M. J. 2001. "Resurgent Mass Partisanship: The Role of Elite Polarization." *American Political Science Review* 95 (3): 619–631.

Hetherington, M. J., and T. J. Rudolph. 2015. *Why Washington Won't Work: Polarization, Political Trust, and the Governing Crisis.* Chicago: University of Chicago Press.

House, T. W. 2013. "Now Is the Time: Gun Violence Reduction Executive Actions." whitehouse.gov.

Huang, H. 2010. "Electoral Competition When Some Candidates Lie and Others Pander." *Journal of Theoretical Politics* 22 (3): 333–358.

Imai, K., and T. Yamamoto. 2013. "Identification and Sensitivity Analysis for Multiple Causal Mechanisms: Revisiting Evidence from Framing Experiments." *Political Analysis* 21 (2): 141–171.

Imai, K., L. Keele, and T. Yamamoto. 2010. "Identification, Inference and Sensitivity Analysis for Causal Mediation Effects." *Statistical Science* 25 (1): 51–71.

Iyengar, S., K. S. Hahn, J. A. Krosnick, and J. Walker. 2008. "Selective Exposure to Campaign Communication: The Role of Anticipated Agreement and Issue Public Membership." *The Journal of Politics* 70 (1): 186–200.

Jacobs, L. R., and R. Y. Shapiro. 1994. "Issues, Candidate Image, and Priming: The Use of Private Polls in Kennedy's 1960 Presidential Campaign." *American Political Science Review* 88 (3): 527–540.

2000. *Politicians Don't Pander: Political Manipulation and the Loss of Democratic Responsiveness.* Chicago: University of Chicago Press.

Jaffe, G. 2015. "Obama Regrets Not Closing Guantanamo on First Day in Office." www.washingtonpost.com/news/post-politics/wp/2015/03/18/obama-regrets-not-closing-guantanamo-on-first-day-in-office/ (published March 18, 2015; accessed June 27, 2020).

Jamieson, K. H., and D. S. Birdsell. 1988. *Presidential Debates: The Challenge of Creating an Informed Electorate.* New York: Oxford University Press.

Jarvis, S. E. 2004. "Partisan Patterns in Presidential Campaign Speeches, 1948–2000." *Communication Quarterly* 52 (4): 403–419.

Johnson, J. 2016. "Here are 76 of Donald Trump's Many Campaign Promises." *Washington Post.* www.washingtonpost.com/news/post-politics/wp/2016/01/22/here-are-76-of-donald-trumps-many-campaign-promises/?utm_term=.a043496e22ea (published January 1, 2016; accessed November 7, 2017).

Just, M. R. 1996. *Crosstalk: Citizens, Candidates, and the Media in a Presidential Campaign.* Chicago: University of Chicago Press.

Just, M. R., A. Crigler, and L. Wallach. 1990. "Thirty Seconds or Thirty Minutes: What Viewers Learn from Spot Advertisements and Candidate Debates." *Journal of Communication* 40 (3): 120–133.

Kaid, L. L., and M. Chanslor. 1995. "Changing Candidate Images: The Effects of Political Advertising." In K. Hacker (Ed.). *Candidate Images in Presidential Elections* Westport, Connecticut. 83–97.

Karol, D. 2009. *Party Position Change in American Politics: Coalition Management.* New York: Cambridge University Press.

Kartik, N., and R. P. McAfee. 2007. "Signaling Character in Electoral Competition." *The American Economic Review* 97 (3): 852–870.

Kasich, J. 2015. "Transcript of the Republican Presidential Debate in Detroit." www.nytimes.com/2016/03/04/us/politics/transcript-of-the-republican-presidential-debate-in-detroit.html (accessed November 7, 2018).

Keen, D. 2012. "Sandy Hook School Shooting, Delivered on Dec. 21, 2012 (Transcript)." www.washingtonpost.com/politics/ remarks-from-the-nra-press-conference-on-sandy-hook-school-shooting-delivered-on-dec-21-2012-transcript/2012/12/21/story.html (accessed on November 10, 2014).

Keneally, M. 2016. "Donald Trump's Evolving Stance on Abortion." http://abcnews.go.com/Politics/donald-trumps-evolving-stance-abortion/story?id=38057176 (accessed November 7, 2017).

Kern, M. 1989. *Thirty-Second Politics: Political Advertising in the Eighties.* New York: Praeger Publishers.

Kerry, J. 2004. "Presidential Debate in St. Louis, Missouri on October 8." *The American Presidency Project.* www.presidency.ucsb.edu/documents/presidential-debate-st-louis-missouri (accessed February 23, 2012).

Kinder, D. R. 1986. "Presidential Character Revisited." *Political Cognition* 19: 233–255.

Kinder, D. R., M. D. Peters, R. P. Abelson, and S. T. Fiske. 1980. "Presidential Prototypes." *Political Behavior* 2 (4): 315–337.

Koger, G. 2003. "Position-Taking and Cosponsorship in the U.S. House." *Legislative Studies Quarterly* 280 (2): 225–246.

Kostadinova, P. 2013. "Democratic Performance in Post-communist Bulgaria: Election Pledges and Levels of Fulfillment, 1997–2005." *East European Politics* 29 (2): 190–207.

2015. "Party Pledges in the News: Which Election Promises Do the Media Report?" *Party Politics* (January).

Kraus, S. 2013. *Televised Presidential Debates and Public Policy.* London: Routledge.

Kronrod, A., A. Grinstein, and L. Wathieu. 2011. "Enjoy! Hedonic Consumption and Compliance with Assertive Messages." *Journal of Consumer Research* 39 (1): 51–61.

Krosnick, J. A. 1988. "The Role of Attitude Importance in Social Evaluation: A Study of Policy Preferences, Presidential Candidate Evaluations, and Voting Behavior." *Journal of Personality and Social Psychology* 55 (2): 196.

1990. "Americans' Perceptions of Presidential Candidates: A Test of the Projection Hypothesis." *Journal of Social Issues* 46 (2): 159–182.

Krosnick, J. A., P. S. Visser, and J. Harder. 2010. "The Psychological Underpinnings of Political Behavior." *Handbook of Social Psychology* 2: 1288–1342.

Krukones, M. G. 1984. *Promises and Performance: Presidential Campaigns as Policy Predictors.* Lanham, MD: University Press of America.

Krupnikov, Y., and J. B. Ryan 2017. "Choice vs. Action: Candidate Ambiguity and Voter Decision Making." *Quarterly Journal of Political Science* 12 (4): 479–505.

Lemert, J. B. 1993. "Do Televised Presidential Debates Help Inform Voters?". *Journal of Broadcasting & Electronic Media* 37(1): 83–94.

Lenz, G. S. 2013. *Follow the Leader?: How Voters Respond to Politicians' Policies and Performance.* Chicago: University of Chicago Press.

Levay, K. E., J. Freese, and J. N. Druckman. 2016. "The Demographic and Political Composition of Mechanical Turk Samples." *Sage Open* 6 (1): 2158244016636433.

Levendusky, M. 2009. *The Partisan Sort: How Liberals Became Democrats and Conservatives Became Republicans.* Chicago: University of Chicago Press.

Lindgren, E., and E. Naurin. 2017. "Election Pledge Rhetoric: Selling Policy with Words." *International Journal of Communication* 11: 22.

Lombard, M., J. Snyder-Duch, and C. C. Bracken. 2002. "Content Analysis in Mass Communication: Assessment and Reporting of Intercoder Reliability." *Human Communication Research* 28 (4): 587–604.

Manin, B. 1997. *The Principles of Representative Government.* Cambridge: Cambridge University Press.

Mansbridge, J. 2003. "Rethinking Representation." *American Political Science Review* 97 (04): 515–528.

2009. "A Selection Model of Political Representation." *Journal of Political Philosophy* 17 (4): 369–398.

2011. "Clarifying the Concept of Representation." *American Political Science Review* 105 (3): 621–630.

Mansergh, L., and R. Thomson. 2007. "Election Pledges , Party Competition, and Policymaking." *Comparative Policits* 39 (3): 311–329.

Mason, L. 2018. *Uncivil Agreement: How Politics Became Our Identity.* Chicago: University of Chicago Press.

Matalin, M., J. Carville, and P. Knobler. 1994. *All's Fair: Love, War, and Running for President,* 1 trade ed. New York: Random House.

Mayhew, D. R. 2004[1974]. *Congress: The Electoral Connection.* New Haven, CT: Yale University Press.

McCain, J. 2008. "Presidential Debate in Hempstead, New York on October 15." www.presidency.ucsb.edu.

McDermott, R. 2011. "Internal and External Validity." In *Cambridge Handbook of Experimental Political Science,* eds. J. Druckman, D. P. Green, J. H. Kuklinski, and A. Lupia. Cambridge: Cambridge University Press, 27–40.

McGillivray, F. 1997. "Party Discipline as a Determinant of the Endogenous Formation of Tariffs." *American Journal of Political Science* 41 (2): 584–607.

McGinnis, J. 1969. "Selling of the President, 1968." New York : Trident Press.

McGraw, K. 2011. "Candidate Impressions and Evaluations." In *Cambridge Handbook of Experimental Political Science,* eds. J. Druckman, D. P. Green, J. H. Kuklinski, and A. Lupia. Cambridge: Cambridge University Press, 187–200.

McGraw, K. M., M. Lodge, and J. M. Jones. 2002. "The Pandering Politicians of Suspicious Minds." *The Journal of Politics* 64 (2): 362–383.

Meirowitz, A. 2005. "Informational Party Primaries and Strategic Ambiguity." *Journal of Theoretical Politics* 17 (1): 107–136.

Merriam-Webster. 2014. "Promise." www.merriam-webster.com/dictionary/promise.

Milita, K., J. B. Ryan, and E. N. Simas. 2014. "Nothing to Hide, Nowhere to Run, or Nothing to Lose: Candidate Position-Taking in Congressional Elections." *Political Behavior* 36 (2): 427–449.

Miller, W. E., and D. E. Stokes. 1963. "Constituency Influence in Congress." *American Political Science Review* 57 (1): 45–56.

Miller, W. E., D. R. Kinder, and S. J. Rosenstone. 1999. *American National Election Studies, 1992 Time Series Study [dataset]*. Ann Arbor: University of Michigan, Center for Political Studies.

Minow, N. N., and C. L. LaMay. 2008. *Inside the Presidential Debates: Their Improbable Past and Promising Future*. Chicago: University of Chicago Press.

Mullinix, K. J., T. J. Leeper, J. N. Druckman, and J. Freese. 2015. "The Generalizability of Survey Experiments." *Journal of Experimental Political Science* 2 (2): 109–138.

Mullis, S. 2012. "Leaked Video Shows Romney Discussing 'Dependent' Voters.". *It's All Politics: Political News from NPR*. www.npr.org/sections/itsallpolitics/2012/09/17/161313644/leaked-video-purports-to-show-romney-discuss-dependent-voters (published September 17, 2012; accessed September 17, 2012).

Naurin, E. 2002. "The Pledge Paradox." *ECPR Joint Session in Turin* (March): 22–27.

———. 2011. *Election Promises, Party Behaviour and Voter Perceptions*. Basingstoke: Palgrave Macmillan.

———. 2014. "Is a Promise a Promise? Election Pledge Fulfilment in Comparative Perspective Using Sweden as an Example." *West European Politics* 37 (5): 1046–1064.

Nielsen. 2016. "Third Presidential Debate of 2016 Draws 71.6 Million Viewers." www.nielsen.com/us/en/insights/article/2016/third-presidential-debate-of-2016-draws-71-6-million-viewers/ (published October 20, 2016; accessed January 20, 2020).

Obama, B. 2012. "Full Transcript of the Second Presidential Debate." *New York Times*. www.nytimes.com/2012/10/16/us/politics/transcript-of-the-second-presidential-debate-in-hempstead-ny.html (accessed August 20, 2013).

Page, B. I. 1976. "The Theory of Political Ambiguity." *American Political Science Review* 70 (3): 742–752.

———. 1978. *Choices and Echoes in Presidential Elections: Rational Man and Electoral Democracy*. Chicago: University of Chicago Press.

Paolacci, G., and J. Chandler. 2014. "Inside the Turk: Understanding Mechanical Turk as a Participant Pool." *Current Directions in Psychological Science* 23 (3): 184–188.

Paolacci, G., J. Chandler, and P. G. Ipeirotis. 2010. "Running Experiments on Amazon Mechanical Turk." *Judgment and Decision Making* 5 (5): 411–419.

Parkin, M. 2014. *Talk Show Campaigns: Presidential Candidates on Daytime and Late Night Television*, vol. 4. New York: Routledge.

Petrocik, J. R. 1996. "Issue Ownership in Presidential Elections, with a 1980 Case Study." *American Journal of Political Science* 40 (3): 825–850.

Petrocik, J. R., W. L. Benoit, and G. J. Hansen. 2003. "Issue Ownership and Presidential Campaigning, 1952–2000." *Political Science Quarterly* 118 (4): 599–626.

Pétry, F., and B. Collette. 2009. *Measuring How Political Parties Keep Their Promises: A Positive Perspective from Political Science*. Do They Walk Like They Talk? Springer 65–80.

Pitkin, H. F. 1967. *The Concept of Representation*. Berkeley: University of California Press.

Polling Report 2014. "Guns." pollingreport.com/guns.htm (accessed July 20, 2014).

Quinnipiac University Poll. 2017. "March 23, 2017 – U.S. Voters Oppose GOP Health Plan 3-1, Quinnipiac University National Poll Finds; Big Opposition to Cuts to Medicaid, Planned Parenthood." https://poll.qu.edu/national/release-detail?ReleaseID=2443 (published March 23, 2017; accessed November 17, 2017).

Rabinowitz, G., and S. E. Macdonald. 1989. "A Directional Theory of Issue Voting." *American Political Science Review* 93–121.

Rallings, C. 1987. "The Influence of Election Programmes: Britain and Canada 1945–1979." In *Ideology, Strategy and Party Change: Spatial Analysis of Post-War Election Programmes in Nineteen Democracies*, eds. I. Budge, D. Robertsonm and Hear. Cambridge: Cambridge University Press, 1–14.

Ryan, P. 2017. On ABC. This Week [video file]. https://twitter.com/ThisWeekABC/status/861211794886361089 (broadcast May 7, 2017; accessed November 17, 2017).

Rehfeld, A. 2009. "Representation Rethought: On Trustees, Delegates, and Gyroscopes in the Study of Political Representation and Democracy." *American Political Science Review* 103 (2): 214–230.

Riker, W. H. 1996. *The Strategy of Rhetoric: Campaigning for the American Constitution*. New Haven: Yale University Press.

Ringquist, E. J., and C. Dasse. 2004. "Lies, Damned Lies, and Campaign Promises? Environmental Legislation in the 105th Congress." *Social Science Quarterly* 85 (2): 400–419.

Rivers, D. 2008. "Understanding People: Sample Matching." Palo Alto: YouGov \ Polimetrix www.websm.org/db/12/16528/Web%20Survey%20Bibliography/Understanding_people_Sample_matching/ (accessed May 18, 2013).

Robinson, S. L., and D. M. Rousseau. 1994. "Violating the Psychological Contract: Not the Exception but the Norm." *Journal of Organizational Behavior* 15 (3): 245–259.

Romney, M. 2012. "Full Transcript of the Second Presidential Debate." www.presidency.ucsb.edu (accessed August 20, 2013).

Rosema, M. 2006. "Partisanship, Candidate Evaluations, and Prospective Voting." *Electoral Studies* 25 (3): 467–488.

Rousseau, D. 1995. *Psychological Contracts in Organizations: Understanding Written and Unwritten Agreements.* Thousand Oaks, CA: Sage Publications.

Royed, T. J. 1996. "Testing the Mandate Model in Britain and the United States: Evidence from the Reagan and Thatcher Eras." *British Journal of Political Science* 26 (1): 45–80.

Royed, T. J., and S. A. Borrelli. 1997. "Political Parties and Public Policy: Social Welfare Policy from Carter to Bush." *Polity* 29 (4): 539–563.

1999. "Parties and Economic Policy in the USA Pledges and Performance, 1976–1992." *Party Politics* 5 (1): 115–127.

Rubio, M. 2015. "Transcript of the Republican Presidential Debate in Detroit." www.nytimes.com/2016/03/04/us/politics/transcript-of-the-republican-presidential-debate-in-detroit.html (accessed November 7, 2018).

Saward, M. 2014. "Shape-Shifting Representation." *American Political Science Review* 108 (4): 723–736.

Schiller, W. J. 1995. "Senators as Political Enrepreneurs: Using Bill Sponsorship to Shape Legislative Agendas." *American Journal of Political Science* 39 (1): 186–203.

Sellers, P. J. 1998. "Strategy and Background in Congressional Campaigns." *American Political Science Review* 92 (1): 159–171.

Shaw, C. M. 1998. "President Clinton's First Term: Matching Campaign Promises with Presidential Performance." *Congress and the Presidency: A Journal of Capital Studies,* 25 (1): 43–65.

Shepsle, K. A. 1972. "The Strategy of Ambiguity: Uncertainty and Electoral Competition." *American Political Science Review* 66 (2): 555–568.

Sides, J. 2006. "The Origins of Campaign Agendas." *British Journal of Political Science* 36 (3): 407.

Sides, J., M. Tesler, and L. Vavreck. 2019. *Identity Crisis: The 2016 Presidential Campaign and the Battle for the Meaning of America.* Princeton, NJ: Princeton University Press.

Slothuus, R., and C. H. de Vreese. 2010. "Political Parties, Motivated Reasoning, and Issue Framing Effects." *The Journal of Politics* 72 (3): 630–645.

Smart Gun Laws. 2014. "Tracking State Gun Laws: 2014 Developments." smartgunlaws.org/tracking-state-gun-laws-2014-developments/ (accessed June 28, 2014).

Sniderman, P. M., and E. H. Stiglitz. 2012. *The Reputational Premium: A Theory of Party Identification and Policy Reasoning.* Princeton, NJ: Princeton University Press.

Stein, R. M., and K. N. Bickers. 1994. "Congressional Elections and the Pork Barrel." *The Journal of Politics* 56 (2): 377–399.

Stokes, D. E. 1963. "Spatial Models of Party Competition." *American Political Science Review* 57 (2): 368–377.

Stokes, D. E. 1966. "Some Dynamic Elements of Contests for the Presidency." *American Political Science Review* 60 (1): 19–28.

Strolovitch, D. Z., J. S. Wong, and A. Proctor. 2017. "A Possessive Investment in White Heteropatriarchy? The 2016 Election and the Politics of Race, Gender, and Sexuality." *Politics, Groups, and Identities* 5 (2): 353–363.

Sulkin, T. 2005. *Issue Politics in Congress.* New York: Cambridge University Press.

2009. "Campaign Appeals and Legislative Action." *The Journal of Politics* 71 (3): 1093–1108.

2011. *The Legislative Legacy of Congressional Campaigns.* New York: Cambridge University Press.

Thomson, R. 2001. "The Programme to Policy Linkage: The Fulfilment of Election Pledges on Socio–economic Policy in The Netherlands, 1986–1998." *European Journal of Political Research* 40 (2): 171–197.

Thomson, R., T. Royed, E. Naurin, et al. 2017. "The Fulfillment of Parties' Election Pledges: A Comparative Study on the Impact of Power Sharing." *American Journal of Political Science* 61 (3): 527–542.

Tingley, D., T. Yamamoto, K. Hirose, L. Keele, and K. Imai. 2013. "Mediation: R Package for Causal Mediation Analysis." *R Package Version* 4 (3).

Tomz, M., and R. P. V. Houweling. 2008. "Candidate Positioning and Voter Choice." *American Political Science Review* 102 (3): 303–318.

2009. "The Electoral Implications of Candidate Ambiguity." *American Political Science Review* 103 (1): 83–98.

Tomz, M., and R. van Houweling. 2012*a*. "Candidate Repositioning." https://tomz.people.stanford.edu/sites/g/files/sbiybj4711/f/tomzvanhouweling-repositioning-2012-10-24.pdf (draft Fall 2012; accessed March 23, 2016).

2012*b*. "Political Pledges as Credible Commitments." https://tomz.people.stanford.edu/sites/g/files/sbiybj4711/f/tomzvanhouweling-pledges-2012-03-27.pdf (draft March 2012; accessed March 23, 2016).

Trump, D. J. 2016*a*. "Presidential Debate in Hempstead, New York on September 26." *The New York Times.* www.nytimes.com/2016/09/27/us/politics/transcript-debate.html (accessed January 10, 2020).

2016*b*. "Presidential Debate in St. Louis, Missouri on October 9." *The New York Times.* www.nytimes.com/2012/10/16/us/politics/transcript-of-the-second-presidential-debate-in-hempstead-ny.htm (accessed January 16, 2020).

Vanberg, C. 2008. "Why Do People Keep Their Promises? An Experimental Test of Two Explanations." *Econometrica* 76 (6): 1467–1480.

VanSickle-Ward, R. 2014. *The Devil Is in the Details: Understanding the Causes of Policy Specificity and Ambiguity.* Albany, NY: SUNY Press.

Vavreck, L. 2001. "Voter Uncertainty and Candidate Contact: New Influences on Voting Behavior." In Communication in U.S. Elections: New Agendas, eds. Roderick P. Hart and Daron R. Shaw. Lanham: Rowman and Littlefield, 91–104.

2009. *The Message Matters: The Economy and Presidential Campaigns.* Princeton, NJ: Princeton University Press.

Vladimirov, N. 2017. "Cook Political Report Moves 20 Districts toward Dems after ObamaCare Repeal Vote." The Hill. https://thehill.com/blogs/blog-briefing-room/news/332062-cook-report-weakens-forecast-for-20-gop-districts-after (published May 5, 2017; accessed November 18, 2017).

Walters, B. 1976. "Presidential Debate in Williamsburg on October 22." www.presidency.ucsb.edu/ ws/index.php?pid=6517;.

Westfall, J., L. van Boven, J. R. Chambers, and C. M. Judd. 2015. "Perceiving Political Polarization in the United States: Party Identity Strength and Attitude Extremity Exacerbate the Perceived Partisan Divide." *Perspectives on Psychological Science* 10 (2): 145–158.

Wittman, D. 1983. "Candidate Motivation: A Synthesis of Alternative Theories." *American Political Science Review* 77 (1): 142–157.

Zaller, J. R. 1992. *The Nature and Origins of Mass Opinion.* New York: Cambridge University Press.

Zinshteyn, M. 2016. "College Freshmen Are More Politically Engaged than They Have Been in Decades." *fivethirtyeight.com* 11: 2016.

Index